RANDOM
HOUSE

LARGE
PRINT

TO *Heaven* AND BACK

A Doctor's Extraordinary Account
of Her Death, Heaven, Angels, and Life Again

A True Story

MARY C. NEAL, MD

RANDOM HOUSE
LARGE PRINT

I dedicate this book to God:

You gave me life

And I live for your glory.

CONTENTS

"This is the beginning of a new day.
God has given me this day to use as I will.
I can waste it or grow in its light and be of
service to others.
But what I do with this day is important
because I have exchanged a day of
my life for it.
When tomorrow comes, today
will be gone forever.
I hope I will not regret the price
I paid for it."

—Anonymous

ACKNOWLEDGMENTS

This book is written with special thanks to:

- Bill Neal, for being my loving, patient, funny, talented, and devoted life partner.

- Willie, Eliot, Betsy, and Peter Neal, for your constant inspiration, wonder, and deep beauty. You are the sources of my greatest joy and most profound sorrow, but my life would be barren without the experience of each of you.

- Ellen Nolan, David Pfeifer, Sophie Craighead, Reverend Dr. Paul Hayden, Terri Hayden, Cindy Leinonen, Mark Barron, Elizabeth Gerdts, and Kasandra Loertscher, without whom our family would not have survived nor be where we are today.

- Tom, Debbi, Kenneth, Anne, Chad, Krista, Tren, and Linzie Long, for bringing me back to earth and for being such a loving part of our family.

- Betty Thum for always giving me unconditional love and support. I pray that I give the same to my own children.

- George Thum, Paulita Neal, Edwin Pounder, Robert Hume, and Bill Hume for all the ways in which you have loved and encouraged me.

- My YaYa sisterhood: Linda Purdy, Susan Farquhar, Kelly Kiburis, Becky Patrias, Julie Connors, Ann Bayer, and Susan Marks, who have sustained me for more than forty years.

- Robin Steinmann, Corrine Alhum, Barb Forbes, Natalie Stewart, and Sherry Pointsett for helping me understand the power of prayer.

- Marta Lozano, for your continued support and for tolerating my working on this book instead of completing my charts.

- All the unnamed people who have helped me become the person that I am today.

PROLOGUE

**"The best and most beautiful things
in this world cannot be seen or even heard,
but must be felt with the heart."**

—Helen Keller

∽

God and His angelic messengers are present and active in our world today and this involvement and intervention is both ordinary in its frequency and extraordinary in its occurrence. Despite leading what I would consider a very ordinary life, I have had the privilege of being touched by God in visible and very tangible ways. One of these experiences began on January 14, 1999, when I was vacationing in South America with my husband. While boating, I was pinned underwater in my kayak and drowned. I died and went to heaven. After a brief stay, I was returned to my body. I returned to my earthly life with two shattered legs and severe pulmonary problems. I was hospitalized for more than a month, wheelchair bound for even longer, and did not return to my orthopaedic surgery practice for more than six months.

Many have described my accident as terrible and tragic. I describe it as one of the greatest gifts I have ever received. The series of events surrounding my accident and recovery were nothing short of miraculous. Not only did I have the privilege of experiencing heaven, but I continued to experience the intensity of God's world and conversed with Jesus several times in the weeks after my return.

Through this experience and conversation, I gained an understanding of many of life's important questions, such as "What happens when we die?", "Why are we here?", and "Why do bad things happen to good people?" I also gained an understanding of the disciple Paul's statement from **1 Corinthians 13** that of faith, hope, and love, the most enduring is love. I already had reasons to believe in miracles, but taking a journey to heaven and back transformed my faith into knowledge and my hope into reality. My love remained unchanged and everlasting.

One of the several reasons for my return to earth was to tell my story to others and help them find their way back to God. During my initial recovery, I was invited to share my story with small groups in my community and these people shared my story with their friends and family. As it was spread to many parts of the country, I was often told of the profound impact my story made on the lives of the people who heard it. In the process of sharing, I realized that my story does not really belong to me, but to God and is meant to be shared. It has inspired many people, stimulated discussion, and has often resulted in a rejuvenated relationship with God. It has lessened people's fear of death and increased their passion for living a full and meaningful life. My story has deepened people's faith and given them hope for the future.

Noblesse Oblige: With Privilege Comes Responsibility

Truly, God does not give us a lamp so we can hide it under a basket or a bed. He gives each of us a lamp so we may give light to the world. Light always dissipates the emptiness of darkness. Ultimately, I felt that if the reading of my story could bring even one person closer to God, it would be worth the writing.

Thus, I began to set down on paper an account of my observations and experiences.

What I could not have known, and did not know as I worked to complete my manuscript, was that the sense of urgency compelling me to complete it was also God's hand at work in my life. For the story did not end there . . .

INTRODUCTION

**"Hear my cry, O God; listen to my prayer.
From the end of the earth I call to you,
when my heart is faint.
Lead me to the rock that is higher than I."**

—Psalm 61:1–2 (NRS)

∾

The tiny two-track road in the remote mountains of Mexico was saturated with rain from the previous night. It was late in the day and we were still several hours from the main road when our dilapidated truck slid off the road and immediately sank into the thick brown mud that formed the shoulder of the road. Our traveling group consisted of the fifteen-year old me, an adult missionary couple, another teenager, and a little baby. Our truck's spinning wheels were unable to gain traction and the truck quickly sank to its axels. Our anxiety level rose quickly, as we knew that it would be a nearly impossible struggle for us to free the wheels of our truck. It was equally impossible for us to walk far enough to find help.

We were not prepared for this sort of delay. The baby would need food and we knew the temperatures would plummet once the sun dipped below the horizon. It was imperative that we get the truck back on the road, as we had driven this desolate stretch of road many times over the summer and had never seen another vehicle. We focused entirely on the task at hand and tried again and again to free the wheels. The depth of the mud seemed to have no limit, and our efforts appeared feeble. As we worked, we began to pray with great fervor and specificity: We prayed that God would "put rock under us," and soon.

The words had barely floated off our lips when we were shocked to see a rusty old pickup truck rumbling up the road. The driver had taken a wrong turn and was trying to find his way to the main road. When told of our predicament, he graciously offered to give us a ride to town. The cab was too small to hold all of us, so we eagerly climbed into the truck bed and laughingly settled onto his cargo . . . of rocks. We were filled with joy at the sight of rock, knowing that our prayers had been heard.

Was this an answer to our specific prayers? Did God, albeit with a sense of humor, intervene in our lives and answer our prayers? Was the truck driver an angel or other messenger of God? Was this a miracle? Maybe it was just luck or a coincidence. A coincidence is defined as the "accidental occurrence of events that seem to have a connection." Luck is a "force that brings good fortune or adversity. It favors chance." For myself, I call it a miracle: an "event that is considered a work of God."

The Bible describes many times when angels are sent by God to help those who are in need; often in times of turmoil, life-threatening situations, or at the moment of death. Miracles appear to be universal and are reported by Catholics, Protestants, Muslims, and Hindus. The Quran describes a miracle as the "supernatural intervention in the life of a human being." The Catholic Church describes miracles as "works of God," usually with a specific purpose, such as the conversion of a person to the faith. **Merriam-Webster's Collegiate Dictionary** defines a miracle as an "extraordinary event manifesting divine intervention."

Cynics claim that miracles defy the laws of nature and, therefore, cannot occur. As described by others who believe as I do, there is a different way to perceive a miracle.

Situation #1
A ball is dropped from a height and falls to the ground. It obeys the laws of nature.

Situation #2
A ball is dropped from a height and falls toward the ground. A hand reaches out and catches it. It never reaches the ground. The ball has obeyed the laws of nature, but the hand has intervened. If the hand were God's, we would have witnessed divine intervention without a defiance of the laws of nature.

I believe that God heard our heartfelt cry on that little road in Mexico and chose to intervene on our behalf. Although the answer was not what we expected, God gave us a specific answer to our specific prayer: He put rock under us.

Over the years, like most people, I have questioned my spirituality. I have wondered about the reality of God, the role of God in my life, wondered why so many bad things are allowed to happen, and wondered about the reality of life after death. Despite these questions and doubts, I witnessed countless numbers of answered prayers and occasions of divine intervention since this high school experience. I drowned while kayaking on a South American vacation and had the great pleasure, privilege, and gift of going to heaven and back. I had the opportunity to converse with angels and ask many questions. I gained much insight. As one result of this adventure, I have also had the opportunity of listening to many other people describe their own spiritual encounters and near-death experiences. Their stories usually begin with their saying, "I've never told anyone about this, because I didn't think they would believe me, but. . . ."

Is God present in our world today? Do miracles still occur? Are there really angels all around us? Does God keep His promises? Is there sufficient reason to live by faith? I believe the answer to each one of these questions is a definitive "yes" and I believe that you will come to this same conclusion as you read about the miracles I have seen and experienced.

CHAPTER 1

THE EARLY YEARS

> " 'For I know the plans I have for you,'
> declares the Lord, 'plans to prosper you
> and not to harm you, plans to give
> you hope and a future.' "
>
> —Jeremiah 29:11 (NIV)

༄

I was born and raised in an ordinary Midwestern town in Michigan. I lived in a middle-class neighborhood with my parents, Bob and Betty, two brothers, Rob and Bill, one sister, Betsy, and a small dachshund named Trinka. My father was a general surgeon and my mother was a homemaker.

I enjoyed a pleasant childhood which, in some aspects, was idyllic. I did not always have everything I wanted, but never lacked for what I needed. Most importantly for any child, I always felt loved by my family. The creek flowing through the back of our property offered me great excitement and opportunity. I spent many hours in and on that creek; ice skating, boating, fishing, swimming, and exploring. I learned about snails, slugs, and leeches. I learned what happens when a dog eats the bacon from a fishing hook, and I learned not to look a snapping turtle in the eye. My best friend and I built an elaborate freshwater clam farm, only to find out later that pearls are made by oysters, not clams. It was great fun and it developed my love for being immersed in the outdoor natural world.

My family attended the local Presbyterian Church, participating in a denomination in which my grandfather, great-grandfather, and great-great-grandfather had been ordained ministers. Our tall, traditional stone church stood proudly on the town square. While the outside was rather formal and not very inviting, its interior arched toward the sky, beautifully displaying large multi-colored stained glass windows. The pews were well-worn and made of a rich and deeply-colored wood. My siblings and I sat through Sunday school and confirmation classes, church services, and the occasional youth group gatherings, but these activities were mechanical and boring to me. Although I willingly attended, these various activities seemed to have little impact on my life.

My brothers and sister and I certainly never developed a relationship with a living, loving God while growing up, and I don't recall ever being expected to incorporate God or Jesus Christ into my daily life or thoughts. God seemed to be a "Sunday thing" and I do not remember my parents discussing spirituality or religion in our home. In many ways, however, they did model a Christian life for their children. My mother was loving, always supportive, and was an active volunteer in numerous service organizations. My father showed great compassion for those who were less fortunate in their circumstances and he was selfless in his profession as a surgeon.

I would often trail behind my father as he checked on his patients in the hospital or when he was called to the emergency room on weekends. I perceived that his was a life of service, in which he was always kind and respectful to others, was not motivated by money, and always put the feelings and needs of others before his own.

As I approached my teenage years, I became more independent and began to hold my own opinions. I discovered that although my father was good at doing activities together, he was not very good at sharing his feelings with me or discussing topics that I considered meaningful or difficult. I adored him in spite of his flaws and was stunned in the spring of 1970 when my parents' relationship crumbled and my mother asked him to move out of our home.

Divorce was still scandalous at that time and I was outraged when my parents' divorce became final in the autumn of 1971. I was in the seventh grade and quickly became a confused and angry adolescent. When confronted by their divorce listing in the newspaper, I could no longer deny that my 1950s-esque image of an all-American family had been exploded. During that period, church attendance was one of the few stable aspects of my life.

My two older siblings were already in college and my brother and I continued to live with my mother in our childhood home. Each Sunday morning, my father would drive me to the local greasy spoon for breakfast, then to Church services. I was still embarrassed, and probably angry, about my parents' divorce, so refused to attend the Presbyterian Church services with him. Instead, we went to the morning service at the local Episcopal Church. We would usually go for a walk after church then return to his apartment to finish the day with a dinner of baked chicken and green beans: the only dinner he ever knew how to make. While I recognized his limitations, I still clung to the fantasy of his returning to my home, and of our family returning to the ideal of my remembered childhood.

My mother was young, attractive, and interesting, so I should not have begrudged her the desire to date, but I did so anyway and tried to disrupt the process in any way possible. Mack was the first guy who was serious about my mom after Dad moved out. One evening when I returned home, I discovered that he managed to eat all of the cookies I had just baked (none of which had been intended for him) and I was furious. I made my opinion clear and I was delighted never to see him again.

George was the next man who successfully captured mom's attention. He was the general manager of the country club where my brothers worked, and they had told him about our mother. After my brothers persistently nudged him to call, a beautiful courtship developed between George and my mother. Although my parent's divorce had long been final, I still hated the concept of my mother having a "boyfriend." To his credit, George was funny, kind, gentle, understanding, and extremely patient. He also gave the best and longest back-scratches known to mankind, which, I might add, was a very successful way to break through my hostility! He loved my mom and he loved her children, so when my mom held a family conference about a year after they started dating and asked for our permission to marry George, it was impossible to deny her that happiness. In my heart, I remained conflicted. George was a decent man, and I thought he would be a reasonable stepfather, but I continued to pray daily for the return of my father and for the return of the life I had known.

Until the very moment in 1973 when the preacher officially declared Mom and George "husband and wife," I continued to pray that my father would arrive to interrupt the wedding ceremony and reclaim his family. When this didn't happen, I concluded that God hadn't listened to my most desperate of prayers and certainly hadn't answered them.

In my disappointment, I discarded the very notion of praying. I was only one very small creature on a planet of more than four billion people; if there really was a God, why should He listen to me or answer my prayers? I decided that my thoughts about an omnipresent God who cares about individuals had likely been a childish and silly belief so I decided to "move on," leaving my beliefs about God behind me.

I was a smart, accomplished, self-confident fifteen-year old young woman. I thought I knew what was best for me and believed that I was capable of creating my own future without divine input. What was unrecognizable to me at that time was how God not only had heard my most desperate plea, but answered it in a way that was greater and more fulfilling than I could ever have imagined. Through my mother's marriage, God gave me a stepfather who was steadfast in his loving, gentle, and gracious manner. George was supportive and respectful. As a parent, he taught me about joy, friendship, and responsibility. He modeled what a loving, respectful marriage looks like, and he became one of the most important influences in my life. God promises that He has plans for us to give us hope and a future and He kept this promise. George coming into my life was definitely not the answer I had prayed for. It was better.

CHAPTER 2

SPINNING OUT
OF CONTROL

**"The future belongs to those who
Believe in the beauty of their dreams."**

—Eleanor Roosevelt

～

Despite George's steadying presence, my life was still in a state of pain and turmoil as I entered high school. Most of my friends were involved with drugs and alcohol, and I was spinning out of control. On a chilly night in March, actually on my mom's birthday, John, Linda, and another friend picked me up in the brand-new Chevy Impala belonging to John's brother. The ink was still wet on John's driver's license, but we encouraged him to drive over some local "rollercoaster hills" on our way to a party in a neighboring town.

Rollercoaster hills are exactly what they sound like . . . they approximate an amusement park ride. If you drive fast enough, your stomach rises into your throat when the car crests the hill. The wintery March roads were icy, and the new vinyl seats in the car were smooth and slippery as we began to fly over the hills. Linda insisted that we use the seatbelts, and the audible click of the belt buckles was barely fading when John lost control of the car. We struck a tree as we began to spin and immediately heard the violent tearing sound of the rear compartment being ripped from the passenger compartment of the car.

The impact with the tree catapulted our car to the opposite side of the road, where the front engine compartment was sheared off by hitting a second tree. The passenger compartment, with the four of us still inside, then rolled several times down an embankment before coming to a rest upside down. Although we were left hanging inverted in the car, suspended by the seatbelts that we had so recently fastened, none of us were seriously injured.

During our rolling descent into the ravine, I clearly and loudly heard God tell me, "I am with you." At that moment, my fear dissolved, and I was even able to marvel at the beauty of the revolving trees and shrubs I saw through the shattering glass window as we tumbled down the hill. This was my first recognizable experience of

God's presence in my life. I marveled at what I had heard and felt but, to be honest, I was quite startled by this experience. I began to consider that God might not be just a "childish and silly belief" after all. For me, God was real, present, and apparently had more of a plan for my life than I seemed to have.

After this event, my life as a teenager was still confusing although I began to view it as being more meaningful, and containing more of a future than I had previously considered. I began to examine the reality of my behavior, my friends, and my choices. I decided that it was time to take my life more seriously and make some changes. I no longer enjoyed "hanging out" with the crowd on Friday nights, and began to spend more time thinking about my future and what was important to me. I contemplated my goals and how I fit into the bigger picture of the world.

I continued to attend services at both the Presbyterian and Episcopal churches, and also began to intermittently attend the Oakland Road Christian Church with my friend Merry Ann. Although I had been baptized as an infant and confirmed in the Presbyterian Church, I chose to undergo a full-immersion baptism during one of the alter calls at the Oakland Road Christian Church. It makes me chuckle to think about this, as I am pretty much of a social introvert. The very idea of my responding to a public altar call and being immersed in a Plexiglas tank set into the front wall of a full sanctuary is enough to make most of my friends laugh out loud. Regardless, I actually did this and the Holy Spirit must have descended upon me, for when I emerged, I felt light as a feather. I was energized, euphoric, and ecstatic. I felt cleansed and reborn; I became a new person. God's promise that "if anyone is in Christ, he is a new creation; the old has gone, the new has come" (**2 Corinthians 5:17, NIV**) was fulfilled.

CHAPTER 3

MEXICO

"Trust in the Lord with all your heart,
And lean not on your own understanding.
In all your ways acknowledge Him,
And He shall direct your paths."

—Proverbs 3:5–6 (NKJV)

∽

Shortly after my baptismal spiritual transformation, I read a church bulletin in which was contained a fundraising notice from an American missionary couple living in the mountains of central Mexico. Although they were not formally trained to do so, this missionary couple was holding Bible camps and running a medical clinic that provided health care to the poverty-stricken people in the mountains surrounding the town of Matehuala, in the state of San Luis Potosi. They were asking for support, and I felt an immediate call to action.

I was fifteen years old, with no money to give the couple and little interest in their evangelical work, but I thought working in a remote medical clinic would be a grand adventure. I immediately contacted the couple, who warmly welcomed my offer of help. Their only questions were, "How quickly can you come?" and "How long can you stay?" I announced my travel plans to my mother and we were able to arrange for me to receive school credit for my service in Mexico.

Everything fell into place quickly, and I departed for Mexico shortly thereafter. It was a good example (retrospectively, of course) of how easily things come together when one is moving in the direction of God's will. It has taken many years to truly learn that when everything seems difficult and feels as though you are swimming upstream, it is usually because you are not following the direction of God's will. When you are doing God's will, everything seems to happen without much effort or many obstacles.

The missionary couple maintained a home in the city of Matehuala, but spent most of their time in a rustic mountain village several long hours away. It was on our way home one day from this mountain village that our truck became stuck in the mud, as I described in my introduction to this book. While in the mountains, we lived in a small farmhouse and this was where we provided food, Bible classes, and medical care to people living in the surrounding region. We offered a range of medical care, from the treatment of head lice and spider or centipede bites, to the fixing of broken bones and the surgical treatment of common problems, such as appendicitis. As rudimentary as it was, these villagers viewed ours as the only medical care available to them. There actually was a regional hospital, but it was many hours away and the villagers said they travelled there only when their condition was so grim as to have no hope of returning alive.

This particular missionary couple was quite desperate for help and seemed to be in a situation that was way over their heads. Upon my arrival, they handed me an outdated medical book and told me that I would be responsible for all obstetrical care, including births—even the occasional cesarean section. I had been looking for adventure and had a lot of self-confidence, but I was definitely not prepared for this level of responsibility and wondered if they misunderstood my qualifications.

When I questioned them, they suggested I pray for guidance.

I suggested they were crazy.

I prayed feverishly during my time in the clinic. I supervised easy deliveries, performed difficult deliveries requiring interventions, and performed cesarean sections. Gratefully, we never lost a child or a mother, despite my limited knowledge, limited experience, and limited equipment.

In taking credit for these successes, I believed that I had been a quick learner, good reader, careful "surgeon," and so on. Later in my life, once I completed medical school and began my professional training to become an accredited surgeon, it became painfully clear to me that my own efforts had little to do with my early successes. I had merely provided the hands through which God could work. The credit for success belonged squarely on God's shoulders and I don't believe all of our patients would have survived without His guidance and intervention.

When I first read the church bulletin that ultimately led me to the Mexican mountains, I had been interested in the medical clinic, but not at all interested in the missionary or evangelical work. I anticipated that the evangelism, the Sunday services, and the Bible camps would be boring and uncomfortable. I believed that spirituality was a private thing and I did not relish the idea of discussing it with others or encouraging their faith. Everyone in the mountain village, including adults and children, attended our Bible camps and I was surprised to discover that their spiritual enthusiasm was both moving and contagious. They had little in the way of material belongings and often had only enough food for one decent meal a day, but they were gracious and quick with their praise and thanksgiving to God for their daily blessings. God was not just a "Sunday thing" for them, and they sang their hymns with genuine joy in their hearts.

It was inspirational to me to see God working in the lives of these remote villagers, and to recognize that these rural people were just as visible and valuable to God as are the very busy and "important" people from big cities. Clearly, there was nothing about their situation that could separate them from God's love. The evangelical aspect of this adventure may have pushed my "comfort zone," but it proved to be anything but boring.

CHAPTER 4

SPIRITUAL REAWAKENING

**"People only see what they
Are prepared to see."**

—Ralph Waldo Emerson

∽

My experiences in the Mexican mountains gave
me a clearer vision of the person I wanted to become and I continued to work toward that vision
as I finished high school. The ritualized worship
services of the Episcopal Church continued to
sustain me and I found that their predictability
gave a sense of stability to my swirling adoles-
cence. The radiance of the sunlit stained glass
windows energized my spirit and the melodic
rhythm of the cantor's voice allowed my soul to
take wing.

When the opportunity arose, I also intermittently attended services at the Presbyterian
Church, the Catholic Church, the Lutheran

Church, and the non-denominational Christian churches in my family's community. I have always appreciated the variety of religious denominations that are present in our world. Their different styles of worship and ways of communicating offer people in different stages of their life and spiritual journeys an opportunity to find the place where they feel most comfortable and a place where their faith can grow.

After high school graduation, I began studying at the University of Kentucky where, despite my deepening spirituality, I rarely attended religious services. It seems that God rarely has a seat at the table in our educational system. No one is ever asked to actively discount their faith or beliefs, but university life just doesn't seem to make room for the spiritual aspects of life and most students just drift away from spirituality. Life for most college students is entirely about the individual; what we are doing, what we think, what we feel, what we want, and what we are planning for our future. Even if we do things during college that are "altruistic," like volunteering, it is usually because it makes us feel good or looks good on our résumé, not really because we feel called to serve.

I intended to apply for medical school upon completing my undergraduate studies, so I mainly focused on my schoolwork, though I also competed as a member of the varsity swim team. Absent any encouragement to think about the spiritual aspect of my life, I gave little time or thought to God in those years. I was basically living in a spiritual desert until I discovered scuba diving.

As an undergraduate, I routinely donated my blood plasma for pocket money. Donating plasma was easy and lucrative, but the more often I donated, the more I began to wonder about the sterility of the donation center, located in a very dirty part of the city. I also thought about the statistically increasing odds that I might accidentally receive someone else's returned red blood cells due to a mistake in the lab. I began to look for other employment options and found a weekend job in the local scuba diving shop. I have always loved everything about water and I spent hours marveling at the images in the underwater photography books sold in the shop. I was awestruck by the beauty and intricacy of God's underwater creations, and quickly fell in love with the abundance and variety of animal life and the brilliance of the colors found in these photos.

I completed my first scuba course and became passionate about the sport. I gave up my paychecks and began working in exchange for equipment.

When the shop sponsored a trip to the Florida Springs, I couldn't wait to go. The drive from Lexington to Florida was long and our group arrived long after dark, but the water was beautiful, calm, and inviting that evening. We novices were so eager to make our first open-water dive that we compelled our instructors to break the first rule of night diving: Never dive at night where you haven't yet dived during the daytime.

We impatiently donned our equipment and enthusiastically jumped into the water. Once under the surface, I stuck to my instructor like glue. We cruised along the bottom and I was thrilled with the splendor of the fish, and the variety of the colors and shapes of the coral. My first open-water dive was living up to all of my expectations and, too soon for me, the air in our tanks neared empty and it was time to surface.

When we inflated our vests and kicked toward the surface, we did not pop through the water's surface as expected, but solidly struck rock. We swam in another direction, and again struck rock. We had inadvertently entered a cave, to which the exit was not obvious.

My instructor and I searched for the opening, but the visibility had been diminished when, in my inexperience, I kicked the bottom of the lake with my fins and raised a cloud of silt. We were running out of air and the tank alarms were echoing. That's when I remembered to pray. I called out to God and I was immediately filled with the feeling of God's presence and the knowledge that He would show us the way out. He would see me through.

When I speak of experiencing God's presence and knowledge that He would show us the way, I don't necessarily mean that He, God, was planning to personally escort us out of the cave. I'm surely not that fanciful. I mean that I felt the manifestation of God's love and grace, and knew that one of His messengers (a spirit, an angel?) would somehow show us the way. This knowledge allowed me to slow my breathing and pray for my instructor's wisdom.

The silt began to clear and we saw several fish darting back and forth before lining up together, swimming in the current. They seemed to beckon us to follow, which we did. We made one last dive down to the bottom of the cave in the direction of the fish, then swam upward and broke through the surface of the lake just as my instructor's air tank emptied completely.

My instructor and I discussed our shared experience at length. He was entirely focused on himself, and was distraught at having lost control of the situation. He felt responsible for the mistakes that were made and what he thought was his poor judgment. He believed that we had survived because of pure luck. He judged himself a failure and proceeded to drink himself into a state of oblivion. For my part, I had a profoundly different response to our survival. I did not believe that luck was involved. I had experienced a profound sense of calm and a knowledge that God was with us in the cave. I believed we had survived because God intervened, even though we had been such knuckle-heads and He essentially had to push us out of the cave.

The experience in the Florida Springs stimulated a reawakening of my spiritual being. I had the intense feeling of being sure that we are all on earth for a reason, and that I had survived because my work on this planet was not yet complete. This left me with a sense of responsibility to seek God's will for my life, and to follow, as best as I could, the path that was being laid before me. This time, I was determined not to relegate God to the background of my life, but to consciously keep Him present in my thoughts and actions.

CHAPTER 5

GOD IS FAITHFUL

**"The Lord bless you and keep you;
The Lord make his face shine upon you and
Be gracious to you;
The Lord turn his face toward you
and give you peace."**

—Numbers 6:24–26 (NIV)

∽

Upon graduation from college in 1980, I moved to Los Angeles, California, to begin my medical training at UCLA. My time in medical school was, predictably, stressful and demanding. The first two years of medical school were spent primarily in the classroom, which was interesting but not very enjoyable. Clinical training began in the third year and I thoroughly enjoyed the time I spent learning about the many areas of medicine and surgery. I soon discovered that I was much more interested in the surgical fields than the medical ones, as I liked to "fix" problems more than I liked discussing them. I elected to spend a block of time learning about orthopaedic surgery and quickly found that I had discovered my niche. I enjoyed the mechanical aspects of orthopaedics and relished the idea of restoring patients' function and increased activity. It was also a fortuitous choice, as I met my future husband while spending time with the orthopaedic team.

Bill graduated from Stanford University's medical school and although he had intended to stay at Stanford for his surgical training, his girlfriend's job lured her, and thus him, to southern California. That story has its own set of "coincidences"; suffice it to say, he was meant to move south. Their relationship dissolved by the time he came to UCLA for some of his orthopaedic surgical training, where my friend, Peggy, and I had been assigned to his same surgical team. I found him to be quite charming and when I was no longer on his surgical team, we began dating. I soon knew that I would be spending the rest of my life with him.

Before completing medical school, I was accepted into a prestigious orthopaedic surgery training program in New York City. This program required two years of general surgical training elsewhere before starting their focused training program to become an orthopaedic surgeon. My relationship with Bill was flourishing, so this arrangement worked well and I was happy to be chosen to stay at UCLA for my first two years of training.

My general surgical training was very intense and left little time for eating or sleeping, let alone for something not directly related to my work. Although I continued to listen for God's will, tried to follow His lead and live according to Christ's directives, it was easy to let God drift into the background of my life. I just really didn't have time for Him.

It was as if I consigned God to the backseat of my car. I wanted Him to be present, but didn't want Him to distract me and I certainly wasn't ready for Him to drive the car. Thankfully, God is patient and God is faithful. He sits in the backseat just waiting for our invitation to move up to the front so that He can steer and press the pedals. If we give him the car keys, He will take us on an unbelievable ride.

That is not to say that there were not small glimpses of God along my journey. Although the medical profession has recently, and somewhat tentatively, recognized the spiritual component of healing and of dying, patients have experienced this connection throughout the ages. I encountered many patients during my training who wanted to tell me about their spiritual experiences. It was usually done apologetically and with a tone of embarrassment, as they did not want to offend me and did not think "medical people" would listen or believe. Science and spirituality were presumed to be incompatible.

I remember Jennifer, a girl who suffered complete liver failure at the age of fourteen. When I began to care for her, she had just undergone liver transplantation. This was at a time when liver transplantation was still being developed, so her prognosis was poor. There were many complications after her surgery and her new liver was not yet working properly.

An important function of the liver is to produce factors that help a person stop bleeding by forming clots, which effectively plug the "breech in the levee." Without these factors circulating in the bloodstream, a patient does not stop bleeding from raw or cut surfaces. In the 1980s, we did not have useful alternatives to these factors, so while we waited for her new liver to start functioning, we gave Jennifer repeated transfusions of whole blood and factor-rich plasma. We returned her to the operating room almost daily, trying to find and control points of significant bleeding.

Keeping her alive was not an easy task and she soon grew tired of the process.

One day Jennifer told me that she was not afraid of dying, but was afraid of what would happen to her parents. Apparently when her liver had initially failed, she tried to explain to her parents that God was with her and loved her, and that He wanted her to "come home." Her parents refused to accept this, so she agreed to undergo liver transplantation.

One day as I prepared her for yet another trip to the operating room, she told me that she would not be coming back. She thanked me for everything we had done for her and told me that her angels were with her so I should not be sad. She told me she was sad for her parents, but it was time for them to "let me go." I listened and accepted the truth of her words. Still, my tears flowed freely later in the day when her heart stopped beating.

CHAPTER 6

AN ATTITUDE OF JOY

**"Set your minds on things above,
not on earthly things."**

—Colossians 3:2 (NIV)

∾

My time at UCLA was passing quickly and when the time for me to go to New York and begin my specialized orthopaedic surgical training neared, three things were clear:

1. Bill and I were meant to spend our lives together.

2. Bill, who had finished his orthopaedic training, had a great job, and whose family lived in Los Angeles, wasn't enthusiastic about moving to New York.

3. Neither of us was interested in a long-distance relationship.

We both decided it would be best if I could stay in Los Angeles for my orthopaedic surgery training. The one problem with this idea was that positions in orthopaedic surgery training programs were highly sought after, were filled long in advance, and were rarely available at the last minute. We met to discuss this with a friend of Bill's family who, at the time, was the chairman of one of the orthopaedic surgery programs in southern California. He was understanding and gracious, but assured me that there would not be any positions available and that my best option would be to complete my training in New York as previously arranged. Bill and I were quite disappointed and left that meeting feeling gloomy.

I did believe that Bill and I were meant to be together, yet I also knew that I did not want to abandon my plans for further surgical training. I gave my worries to God and asked Him for guidance. A few days later, I was told that one of the young surgeons in the orthopaedic training program at the University of Southern California was unexpectedly taking a leave of absence and there might be a position available. I immediately called, sent my résumé, and was subsequently invited for an interview.

One of the questions asked by the panel of interviewers was, "What is the last book you read?"

This is a pretty standard question and one that most people, including me, would usually try to answer in a way that might show some intellect or highlight an unusual interest. I had recently been vacationing and read **The Hobbit** or some such book of fiction. Try as I might, I could not think of any other books that might seem more impressive to the interviewing panel. I sheepishly told them the title of the book and made a comment to the fact that I had been on vacation and that the book was "nothing important, just fantasy."

I was given the job position and later was jokingly asked if I had been able to read the minds of the interviewers. One of the people on the panel told me that before meeting me, they had already interviewed a number of candidates for the position. They asked each candidate the same question about which book they had most recently read, and each one responded with the name of some sort of intellectually challenging book that seemed unrealistic, considering each candidate was in the midst of surgical training. Just before I walked in they had exasperatedly wished among themselves that a candidate, for once, would just say that the last book he or she had read was nothing but fantasy.

The Los Angeles County Hospital is part of the USC system and provides care to the indigent population. Throughout my training, I cared for many people who existed on the fringe of society, those that were incarcerated, and others who were just trying the best they could to make their part of the world better for all. Similar to my observations in the mountains of Mexico, it was clear that nothing separates these people, or **any** people, from God's promises or love if they just ask that God's door be opened to them.

I certainly learned a great deal during my time at USC and one life lesson that I still think about from time to time came from an unlikely source. The old Los Angeles County Hospital had one central bank of elevators serving thirteen floors of constant activity. Each elevator had its own operator, who organized the occupants and pushed the buttons for their requested floors. The operators were usually quite territorial and swatted away the hands of people who tried to push the buttons themselves. It was a thankless job, as everyone was in a hurry and none of the young doctors, including me, understood why someone else was needed to push the buttons.

There was one elevator operator who arrived by 6 A.M. each day with a large smile on her face and obvious joy in her heart. She was always like a beacon of light in that dark and gloomy building, and many of us would wait longer just to

ride in her elevator. She was old, wizened and un-
educated. She was often treated rudely. But she
never let anyone or anything darken her day, and
she shared her joy with anyone who cared to receive it.

Over my years at USC, I developed respect,
admiration, and a little envy for this elderly operator's world view. One day I asked her how she
was always able to maintain such a rosy outlook.
She told me that her joy and strength came from
the Lord. She knew the only part of life she could
control was her reaction to it, so she chose to
react with love.

I was reminded of her comments many years
later when I asked one of the operating room
nurses in the hospital where I worked in Wyoming how she could possibly work for her current supervisor and administrator (both of whom
were making life quite difficult for the operating room nurses). She just looked at me and said,
"I don't work for them." When I questioned her
further, she replied, "I don't work for her (the
current operating room director) or for him (the
administrator of the hospital). I work for God."

Point made.

CHAPTER 7

GOD SHOUTS WHEN NECESSARY

"We are either in the process of resisting God's truth or in the process of being shaped and molded by His truth."

—Charles Stanley

~

By the summer of 1991, I was thirty-three years old, had a husband, one child, Willie, and was about to give birth to our second child, Eliot. I had completed twelve years of high school, four years of college, four years of medical school, one and a half years of general surgery training, five years of orthopedic surgery training, and one and a half years of specialty training in trauma and spinal surgery. Mentally, emotionally, and professionally—on every level—I was more than ready to begin my "real" life. Within the context of our rapidly expanding family, I felt I could finally set my own goals and control my own future. I accepted a position as the director of spinal surgery at the University of Southern California, as I enjoyed teaching and enjoyed the complexity of the surgical cases that are common in a university setting.

The university environment was exciting, stimulating, and ego gratifying. My position there was entirely satisfying to me for several years, and it seemed that my life was reasonably well balanced. With the help of Dawn, our delightful live-in nanny, who nurtured our kids during the day, Bill and I were both able to freely pursue our careers during the work-week. Our evenings and weekends were completely devoted to spending time with our children, and we savored every minute. We lived by the ocean, so often took them to the beach or sailing. We had barbeques in the sand, visited the museums, and taught them how to ride bicycles. Bill's parents, who lived nearby, would visit frequently, and the kids adored them. On the weekends, we would often drive several hours to our cabin in the mountains north of Los Angeles. There we would kayak, build forts with the kids, swim, and just relax. I would say that we were quite content with the way our lives were evolving.

The time demands on me to teach, develop a medical practice, perform research, publish scientific papers, attend meetings, and commute more than two hours each day began to take its toll after several years. Rather than spending my best time and energy nurturing my relationship with God, my marriage, and encouraging my children, I began to feel that my job claimed most of my life. My children were beginning to blossom into the people they would become, and I did not want to merely be a distant observer. My long commute to downtown Los Angeles meant that I was rarely able to attend daytime school functions, and could never attend on short notice. This also meant that I had very little time or energy to think about the role God played in my life or how I fit into God's plan. I had made a commitment to keep God in the foreground of my life and I did not feel like I was fulfilling this adequately.

I find this to be a commonly shared reality of young people and young families. To paraphrase what my minister once wrote: "We are constantly bombarded by those who want a piece of us; seeking our time, talents, and energy. Sometimes we weary of those demands and, at times, we feel God's call on our lives as just another pull when we already feel pulled apart."

Another commonly shared reality, to which many, many women can attest, is the difficulty of being a working mother. Today, women are told they can be anything and achieve everything while simultaneously being great wives, great mothers, and great people. Women have convinced themselves that they can and should be "superwomen," which is exactly what they would have to be in order to do everything well. Reality is always a compromise. There are only twenty-four hours in a day and everyone must prioritize their work responsibilities, family needs, and personal desires in order to decide where and how to make sacrifices. Appropriately prioritizing these various aspects of life is challenging since the right balance point is constantly shifting as a woman moves from one phase of life to another. I think it is healthy and essential to re-evaluate this balancing act occasionally and make changes when needed.

Early in 1993, after I gave birth to our third child, Betsy, I began to reflect on the course of my life (What else is there to do during the many long hours of nighttime baby feeding?). I clearly saw God's fingerprints and influence in my earlier experiences with surviving the car crash as a teen, my service in Mexico, the scuba diving incident in the cave, and elsewhere, and began to wonder whether or not I was truly following God's plan for my life. We attended the United Methodist Church, attracted by their doctrinal social creed that demonstrates a commitment to environmental stewardship, human rights, justice, and seeking peace in the world, but I didn't think that was enough. The spiritual welfare of my children was of critical importance to me and I wanted them not only to attend church services, but also to make their own commitment to God and experience a daily relationship with a living God.

I realized that my life was beginning to tip out of balance. Not only was I becoming increasingly convinced that if I stayed in academic practice, I could not prioritize my life the way I wanted it to be, but the secular environment of the university increasingly began to weigh on me. Not only did I want balance, I wanted the various aspects of my life to be fully integrated. My spiritual yearnings did not match the desire for ego, power, and/or money that most of the other faculty members seemed to have. Despite feeling more and more disjointed, I nonetheless found it difficult to leave my job. I knew what to expect in that environment, and was not sure that the situation would be any different or better elsewhere. For me, like for most people, a known situation, however unpleasant, is often more comfortable and easier to accept than the fear of an unknown one.

In hindsight, I can see many ways in which God had been calling to me and asking me to change the direction of my life. Because I didn't listen, He had to shout.

New surgeons began to join our orthopaedic department and this resulted in my working environment becoming increasingly less compatible with my vision for my life. One day in 1996, my chairman hired a new surgeon to join my section of the department. I had raised concerns about his qualifications, but my chairman had been bamboozled by this surgeon's previous employers. This new surgeon, who was on the verge of retirement, had an impressive résumé, but I found him to be languid and dull. We were definitely not compatible and I questioned my ability to spend the necessary time with him.

Not long after his arrival, we spent a family vacation in Northern Michigan. Bill's grandfather was a professional cellist who taught each summer at the Interlochen Arts Academy, so Bill's mother had spent most of her summers enjoying this part of Michigan. Not surprisingly, Bill and his brothers had also spent their youthful summers in Interlochen. In keeping with this generational tradition, Bill, his parents, our children, and I traveled to Interlochen and had a delightful time swimming in the lake, picking blueberries, rolling down the sand dunes, and sharing many laughs. One afternoon, we stopped in to visit the

Traverse City Pie Company. This was a new business and I had discovered that the owner, Denise, was a friend I had known when we were both in high school. She and I had been on the swim team together and had shared our Christian faith. Bill returned to the cabin with our kids, leaving Denise and me to spend the warm afternoon chatting and eating pie. As we caught up on our lives, we talked about many things, including my high school commitment to Christ.

After she drove me back to my family's little cottage, I contemplated my loving husband and our beautiful children, including Peter, our fourth child who was just beginning to form in my womb. I reflected on my conversation with Denise and my continuing desires for complete integration of my life. Until that moment, it seemed that I had done a lot of thinking and contemplating with regard to my spirituality, my desire to put God and my family at the top of my priority list, and so on, but not much in the way of action.

This part of the story is probably starting to sound familiar. You know the one I am talking about . . . thinking about something, making a commitment to change, failing in the commitment, making a new commitment to change, failing again . . . On and on the cycle goes. Fortunately for all of us, God is very, very patient. He will continue calling to us, He will shout when He must, and He will always welcome us back with loving, nonjudgmental arms.

At that moment, although I felt like the prodigal son asking for yet another chance, I renewed my commitment to living a Christ-centered life and renewed my commitment to placing the needs of my family above those of my career. I had no idea just what this meant for me until I attended an unusually boring faculty meeting after returning to Los Angeles.

Rather than listening to the tedious agenda, I spent this time reflecting on each faculty member present. As I considered the people in the room, I thought about what I knew of each person's life. Other than my chairman, most of the men were divorced, having affairs, were heavy drinkers, or had kids with their own brand of problems. I then considered my own life and knew that I didn't want my future to be in this sort of environment.

That evening as I made my final decision to leave the University, I was simultaneously overcome with grief and exhilaration. I knew I would be sorry to leave my chairman, as I had great respect and fondness for him and did not want to disappoint him, but I was exhilarated by the idea of being free from the bonds of my job. I was desperate to leave and eagerly called my chairman the next morning, asking him how soon I could be released from my obligations.

I left the university within a month, joined my husband's orthopaedic group, and was deeply grateful to God for shouting at me when I would not listen to His calling. Looking back, I was able to recognize the series of events and "coincidences" that represented the increasingly insistent calling of God for me to make this decision.

CHAPTER 8

BREAKING THE BONDS

**"A man's heart plans his course,
But the Lord directs his steps."**

—Proverbs 16:9 (NKJV)

༄

Although Bill had grown up in Los Angeles, we had never really planned to stay in Southern California. We lived in Los Angeles in order to be close to Bill's family, but his brothers had recently moved to other states and his parents were planning to retire and move north. Leaving my job at USC not only freed me from academic medicine, it also freed my family from the final bond that tied us to Los Angeles. I had redefined my personal priorities and now our family had the opportunity to do the same. Bill and I both wanted to move to a place that was smaller than Los Angeles and where our children could experience nature on a daily basis without the need to drive several hours to do so.

We sat down and made a Venn diagram of the places where I would like to live and those where Bill would like to live. A Venn diagram consists of overlapping circles that represent different groups. The overlapping portions of the circles represent the common characteristics of the two groups. The Venn diagram of our potential living locations looked something like this . . .

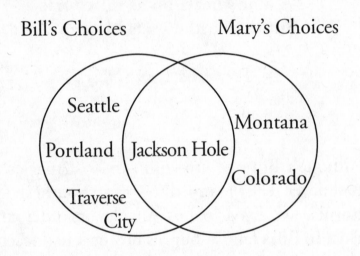

Bill's Choices   Mary's Choices

Seattle

Portland   Jackson Hole   Montana

Traverse   Colorado
City

Our family enjoyed being out-of-doors and being physically active with biking, kayaking, sailing, camping, skiing, and many other sports, so we were looking for a scenic place that offered great recreational opportunities, clean air, and a healthy environment in which we could raise our children. In comparing our preferences, we found that the only overlapping choice was Jackson Hole, Wyoming. Jackson Hole is a delightful valley surrounded by towering granite mountains, beautiful rivers, lakes, forests, and abundant wildlife. A somewhat rural area, with approximately 20,000 full-time residents, it offers world-class winter and summer sports and we thought it would offer a safe and loving community in which to raise our children. It was also, unfortunately, not the sort of town with much opportunity for two additional orthopaedic surgeons. We looked at our Venn diagram again, and decided to remain in Los Angeles. As I said earlier, we were not unhappy and by this time, I had learned to "let go and let God." I was confident that when ready, God would show us the plans He had for us.

Several weeks after making this decision, Bill was absent-mindedly flipping through a medical journal when he came upon an advertisement for Jackson Hole. The local orthopaedic group was looking for a spine surgeon to join them. Bill hesitated just a bit before showing me the advertisement, as he had an inner feeling that this one action would change our future. As soon as he showed it to me I applied for the position, interviewed with the partners, and was offered a job. Less than four months later, we were heading to Wyoming loaded up with cars, boats, kids, and cats.

We immediately fell in love with our new community. The people were dynamic, welcoming, and supportive and the outdoor recreational opportunities were abundant. We dove headlong into our "new" life, and took pleasure in watching our kids also embrace the many new opportunities. Just before our move to Wyoming, Willie, our nine-year-old oldest child, and Bill attended a kayaking camp in California where they were befriended by the course organizer, Tom Long.

Tom and his wife, Debbi, had grown up in Southern California, but moved to Boise, Idaho, in the early 1970s. In 1975, they took over the Cascade Raft and Kayak Company on the Payette River. When we first met them, their three sons were impressive teenage paddlers, enjoying much success on the international level. Kenneth and Chad competed together in C-2 races (whitewater and slalom racing in a two-person, closeddeck canoe), while Tren competed individually in a closed-deck kayak. In order for the boys to have access to winter training opportunities, the Longs began spending winters kayaking in South America on the rivers of Chile. As a means to defray some of the cost of this lifestyle, they began to organize Chilean river trips for American clients.

As our relationship with the Longs grew deeper, Bill and I spent more time talking about going to Chile with them. We were both quite fond of the entire Long family and thoroughly enjoyed the time we spent paddling with them on the Payette River. In the summer of 1998, I finally thought all the kids were old enough for us to leave the country without them, so I decided to take Bill kayaking in South America as a special present for his January birthday.

CHAPTER 9

AN ADVENTURE
IN CHILE

**"Moreover, no man knows
when his hour will come."**

—Ecclesiastes 9:12 (NIV)

∾

In January 1999, Bill and I left our children in the capable hands of our nanny and flew from our wonderful Wyoming winter to the delightful Chilean summer. This was our first trip "alone" since Peter's birth and we were looking forward to a terrific adventure. We flew into Temuco, which is about seven hours south of Santiago and about one hour north of our destination of Pucón.

Pucón is a resort-destination town on the shores of the deep and beautiful Lake Villarica, thriving in the shadow of the 9,315-foot Villarica volcano. It is in the heart of Chile's IX Region, the

Lake District. This region is populated by multiple glacier-topped volcanos, providing clear, cool water to the many rivers that form these beautiful lakes.

We stayed in a rental house with the Longs who, at that time, consisted of; Tom and Debbi, Kenneth, their twenty-year-old son, and his wife, Anne, Chad, their eighteen-year-old son, and Tren, their sixteen-year-old youngest son.

We spent a delightful week with Tom, kayaking on the rivers and playing in the whitewater of southern Chile. Bill and I were already proficient kayakers, but we continued to work on our Eskimo rolls, our boating skills in pushy and steep water, and we paddled a number of both scenic and challenging rapids. We also practiced our Spanish, absorbed the wonderful culture, and enjoyed the lake, the town, and the exquisite scenery. Evenings were spent chatting around a blazing fire after first walking into town for ice cream. The time was thoroughly relaxing and we were sad to realize that the end of our trip was quickly approaching.

We began to make plans for our final day of boating, which was to be on the Fuy River with Tom, Kenneth, Chad, Anne, several Americans with whom we had never boated, and a young

Chilean man who was working for the Longs that summer.

The Fuy is a river in the Southern Chilean Los Ríos Region that drains from the northern end of Lake Pirihueico and winds along the northern foothills of the Choshuenco volcano before joining the Neltume River to form the Llanquihue River, which then empties into the glacial Panguipulli Lake. Bill and I are experienced kayakers and have paddled many challenging rivers in the United States, so we were looking forward to our run down the upper section of the Fuy, which is known for its tropical beauty and array of challenging waterfalls—drops of ten to twenty feet, making them exciting but well within our paddling skills.

We first drove to the small village of Choshuenco (population 625) near the shores of Panguipulli, then further to the river put-in. This was a remote area of very sparse population, thick forest, and no development. Once on the river, there really wouldn't be the option to stop paddling or get off the river, so when Bill quite unexpectedly awoke that morning with significant back pain, he decided not to boat.

Although it was a typical sunny, warm Chilean day, I didn't have a good feeling about the trip. I am not a socially graceful person, so assumed it was just my underlying awkwardness and unease of being in a group of new people. Retrospectively, Anne also had a sense of great unease. She wasn't sure why she felt this way. At the time, she thought she was uncomfortable because she was not totally familiar with this river and we were putting on the river later than we had planned, or maybe because it was a group of people who had not previously boated together. Regardless of the reason, she felt a generalized sense of stress.

Bill dropped us off at the put-in, where we met up with the other Americans, and there were joking comments made about being able to see me easily because I was wearing my husband's bright red drytop instead of a more subdued color of paddling shirt. There was some expected anxiety about the anticipated waterfalls and the possibility of boaters making flat landings, as this can cause a broken back. So there were also comments made to the effect that we would be in good company since I am a spine surgeon. As we put on the river, Chad called out to my husband, "We will bring back your wife, and she won't be an inch shorter" (humorously implying that I wouldn't compress my spine with any flat landings). Bill drove off in the truck, intending to find a sunny spot in which to spend the day reading. He planned to meet us at the take-out later in the day.

As our group started down the river, there didn't seem to be any clear boating order, but I tried to stay away far from one particular boater who seemed to have limited skills, no sense of boundaries, and made me feel very apprehensive. I disregarded my apprehension, as it was a beautiful afternoon and I was excited about the upcoming waterfalls.

We approached the first significant drop not long after putting on the river and stopped in an eddy (an area of slow water that is usually downstream of a rock or next to the shore) to discuss how we should run it. There was a narrower channel to the right side of the river and a larger main channel to the left. We decided to run the smaller channel, as it was more predictable and straight forward. The main drop had a tremendous amount of flow, with a steep drop and large hydraulics at its bottom.

Boater number one paddled toward the channel on the river right, but approached with too much angle and her boat became lodged sideways between the two large boulders flanking the drop. Although her boat was stuck, she was able to exit her boat and flush into the pool of calm water below the drop. I had already exited the eddy and was unable to stop my forward progress when I saw her boat blocking our chosen route, so paddled further to the left.

As I paddled forward, the boater who I had been trying to avoid and who had been behind me, washed out of the upper eddy and then bounced ahead of me. She bobbled a bit before going over the main drop backward. Unknown to me, her boat became lodged in the rocks below the turbulence of the main drop. She was able to exit her boat and swim to a rock in the middle of the pool below. I was unaware of her predicament and had few options, so I continued paddling.

As soon as I crested the top of the waterfall, I saw nothing but trouble and knew I was going to have a problem. A big problem. There was a tremendous volume of water flowing through this channel, causing the water at the bottom to be chaotic and violent. I saw a large hydraulic formed by the churning waves and saw no exit. I took a very deep breath and dropped down the waterfall and into what would become a great adventure.

Despite the volume and power of the falling water, her boat prevented any hope of making a clean exit. As my boat rocketed down, the front dove under the other boat and became pinned between it and the submerged rocks of the waterfall. The water immediately engulfed me, my boat, and the previously pinned boat. I was upright in my boat, but the water was flowing over the top of me. My boat and I were essentially buried under both falling water and the other boat. The force of the water was so great that I felt like a rag doll. My body was forced onto the front deck of my boat, with my arms helplessly being pulled downriver.

Anne paddled into the channel on the right, knocked the broached boat loose, and continued into the pool below. Chad went down the main channel. The water was so deep in this drop that he didn't see or feel anything as he paddled down the drop and right over the two boats (and me) that were submerged at the bottom.

As Chad and Anne entered the pool below, they noted boater number one swimming in the water, and easily located her boat which had been dislodged from the right channel. They were then surprised to see a second swimmer (this was the boater whose boat was on top of mine), but could not immediately locate her boat. Chad quickly paddled into an eddy to further evaluate the situation. He could see boater one. Her boat had been dislodged by Anne, and he easily located it on the river bank. He also could see the second boater sitting on a rock in the middle of the river, but he could not immediately locate her boat. At last, he finally caught a glimpse of her red boat at the bottom of the main channel.

It was difficult for Anne and Chad to account for everyone as, at this point in time, our group of paddlers was split: some of the boaters were below the drop and some were still above the drop. It took several minutes and several head counts before Anne was firmly convinced that both my boat and I were missing. Familiar with emergency situations, she started her watch.

CHAPTER 10

DEATH ON THE RIVER

**"Even though I walk through the valley
of the shadow of death,
I shall fear no evil.
For you are with me;
Your rod and your staff, they comfort me."**

—Psalm 23:4 (NIV)

∽

A person paddling a whitewater kayak is held in the kayak by a combination of their spray skirt and the tight fit of their body inside their boat. A spray skirt is a neoprene sheet that encircles a kayaker's waist, stretches to the boat's deck, and forms a tight fit around the cockpit in order to keep water out of the boat. A strip of fabric known as a "grab loop" is sewn to the front edge of the spray skirt, where it wraps around the cockpit. When it is necessary to exit the boat, the paddler can "pull the chute," or, in other words, pull up on the grab loop to release the spray skirt from the deck of the boat, thereby allowing the paddler to use his legs to push himself out of the boat.

When I first realized that I was pinned in the waterfall, I did not panic and I did not struggle, but I desperately tried to get out of my boat by using some standard techniques.

I repeatedly and forcefully tried to reach the grab loop of my spray skirt, but the power of the water forcing my arms downstream was too great and my attempts were laughable. I tried to push against the foot braces. I tried to jiggle the boat. I thought about my family and desperately tried to raise my head out of the water in search of air. I quickly realized that I was not in control of my future.

God had saved me more than once in the past so I, once again, reached toward God and asked for His divine intervention. I did not demand rescue. I knew that He loved me and had a plan for me. I asked only that His will be done. At the very moment I turned to Him, I was overcome with an absolute feeling of calm, peace, and of the very physical sensation of being held in someone's arms while being stroked and comforted. I felt like I imagine a baby must feel when being lovingly caressed and rocked in his mother's bosom. I also experienced an absolute certainty that everything would be okay, regardless of the outcome.

I thought about my husband and young children, about the Longs, and about my life on earth. I thought about my relationship with God. I was grateful that He was holding me and marveled at the intense physicality of this feeling. I easily recalled a long-forgotten poem that hung on the wall of the home of a childhood friend. I had absent-mindedly read it each time I entered my friend's house and now understood its words. The poem was "Footprints in the Sand" by Carolyn Joyce Carty. I have since purchased framed copies that hang in my home and on my office wall. I continue to read these words almost every day:

One night a man had a dream.
He dreamed he was walking along the beach with the Lord.

Scenes from his life flashed across the sky
And he noticed two set of footprints in the sand,
One belonging to him and the other to the Lord.

When the last scene of his life had flashed before him,

He recalled that at the lowest and saddest
times of his life
There was only one set of footprints.

Dismayed, he asked, "Lord, you said that
once I decided to follow you,
You'd walk with me all the way.
I don't understand why, when I needed you
most,
You would leave me."

The Lord replied, "My precious child.
I love you and would never leave you.
During your times of trial and suffering,
When you saw only one set of footprints . . .

That was when I carried you."

Although I felt God was present and holding
me, I was still entirely conscious of my predicament and my surroundings. I was able to feel the
current pushing and pulling my body and feel
the pressure of the water. I could not see anything
or hear anything but I was acutely aware of everything that was happening around and within me.
I was comfortable, calm, and marveled at God's
presence.

When I no longer felt myself trying to breathe,
I assumed that I would die. My thoughts returned

to my husband and children and as I pondered what would become of them without my presence as a wife and mother, I was deeply and profoundly reassured that they would be okay; even if I died.

As I waited under water, I thought about and analyzed my life; its course, my choices, my joys, and my regrets. I thought about everything. Eventually, I thought about how bored I was. I was tired of thinking and tired of waiting; I was ready to get on with the journey, whatever that was meant to be. With the assurance that all would be okay regardless of the outcome, I found myself impatiently urging God to "Hurry up."

CHAPTER 11

MY RESCUE

**"With man, this is impossible,
but not with God.
All things are possible with God."**

—Mark 10:27 (NIV)

〜

While I was experiencing profound comfort, peace, and boredom, the rest of my companions were not so tranquil. When Chad realized I was missing, he frantically looked for my boat. He climbed out of his boat and began to scurry upstream. Tom was boating "sweep" when he saw his son jump onto a rock. He called out to Chad, only to be told that there was one boat stuck, and I and my boat were both missing. Tom was insistent, saying, "Boys, you have to find her!"

As Chad reached the rock ledge above and near the main channel, he saw what he thought was the red of my helmet. The call went out and within a minute, Tom, Chad, and Kenneth were all surveying the situation from the same ledge. They could see my helmet, but there was about four feet of deep, strong current between the ledge upon which they were standing and me. The water was too deep and fast moving for any-one to stand in it, and the gap was too wide to step across or span. It was a classic example of the phrase "so close, yet so far."

Chad held Tom as Tom tried to lean across the gap. Tom then tried to jump the gap in order to grab my boat. He succeeded only in being flushed under my boat and into the pool below.

Again and again they were unsuccessful in their attempts to reach me, and each attempt brought increased yelling and a rising sense of desperation, despair, and discouragement. Noth-ing seemed to be working. Tom describes every-one in our group, including Chad and Kenneth, as being in a state of "tragic terror."

Anne and the other kayakers sat in the pool below consumed by a feeling of total helplessness and mounting hopelessness. The Longs are well versed in, and quite experienced with whitewater rescue, but this was different. Not only was it me, their friend, who was in peril, but they seemed to be making no appreciable progress toward a successful rescue. Nothing they did seemed to work. Time seemed to bend and stand still.

When Tom surfaced after another failed attempt to reach me, he heard Chad yelling, "Hurry, hurry." It had been a number of minutes and they were all aware of the importance of speed. This was quickly becoming the work of body recovery rather than rescue. The boys desperately tried to think of something that would help, including ways to divert the water so that they could reach my boat. As Tom neared total despair, he climbed back onto the rock and felt the scene totally change. The situation seemed to shift, like a light switch being clicked.

He felt like they had spent five or more minutes imitating the Keystone Cops, then suddenly it was different. He felt the atmosphere shift and felt the physical proximity of God. Tom had the distinct feeling that God was saying to them, "You guys are pathetic. Nothing you are doing is going to work, so I had better get involved." Tom felt as if time shifted and God was taking control. Trying to express this to Chad, Tom said, "This has got to be supernatural." Chad thought that his dad meant that his efforts needed to be supernatural, so he reassured Tom that he was trying as hard as possible. Tom told him, "No, not that. I mean this really must be supernatural."

Things began to happen.

They looked down and a dry rock suddenly appeared in the middle of the water flow that separated them from me. They were able to step onto this rock and use it as a platform from which they could reach my boat. Chad was then able to straddle the rocks and securely grip my boat. He had solid footing and was pulling downstream. He was a young, strong, world-champion athlete and everything was aligned for success. He thought to himself, "This will be the time that superhuman strength will kick in, like the woman who is suddenly able to lift the car off of her child."

He pulled forcefully with all of his strength and with the absolute belief that he would be successful. Nothing happened. He felt that if anything was going to work, this is when it would have worked. It didn't. Chad felt totally inadequate and felt that he, and they, had failed me. Kenneth said they tried again and again to move my boat, but it was stuck—really stuck.

Kenneth, Chad, and Tom felt totally helpless with the realization that they could not move my boat. They each noted that only God's intervention would make a difference and, as they reached for my boat one more time, Tom describes feeling a "sonic boom without the sound." My boat rolled a little bit and suddenly Chad was in the water.

During this "sonic boom," my boat shifted slightly, moving my body more fully into the current. The force of this current ripped off my lifejacket and helmet, and then sucked me out of my boat and down the river.

No one saw me exit the boat, but Chad caught a glimpse of something red downstream. He thought it was my lifejacket and sadly thought he should retrieve it for my family. He dove in and grabbed my lifejacket as it bobbed to the surface. As he held my empty lifejacket, he felt my body bump into his legs. He hadn't even known I was there. He reached into the water, grabbed my wrist, and hung on tightly.

Anne, still in her boat, paddled over to help him swim my purple, bloated, oxygen-starved body to the shore. My eyes were devoid of life.

The Longs teach water rescue courses, so they are often the first people called to the scene of an accident on the Payette River. Mine would not have been the first dead body they recovered from a river, but Chad was devastated. Later on he told me this was because he had "watched someone I love die," and he felt that they had utterly failed me. Tom said the atmosphere felt "crushing—like being in the middle of a big car crusher."

They dragged my body to the rocky river bank, where Tom, Chad, and Kenneth began systematically to move through the standard steps of evaluation and resuscitation. Eleven to fourteen minutes had passed since Anne had started her watch, and the atmosphere was gloomy as they began CPR. Tensions were heightened when one woman insisted that they should not revive me, as "she will just be a vegetable," and another boater wanted to videotape the whole event.

One usual teaching of resuscitation is the need to detach oneself emotionally from the specific individual being resuscitated and focus entirely on the CPR protocols until the individual is either revived or pronounced dead.

Contrary to their teaching and experience, Tom, Kenneth, and Chad were never able to let go of the fact that it was I, their friend, who was being resuscitated. While they went through the steps of CPR, they continually prayed for my return and continued calling to me, "Mary, you cannot leave us. We know you are here. Come back. Please take a breath," again and again. They felt as though time had stopped.

When I finally took a very large gasping breath, they were not sure whether it was a recovery breath or merely agonal breathing, the kind of gasping that usually heralds an approaching death. When this breath of mine was not immediately followed by a second one, they called to me again and pleaded for me to take a breath. I followed that repeated call with another single, labored breath and then stopped. They resumed their calling, and again I rewarded them with a single, gasping breath. This pattern continued again and again.

Each time I took a breath, their emotions rose to "total lightness." Each time I stopped, they sunk into "total darkness." Each breath returned their sense of time to "normal." Each time I stopped, time stood still for them.

Occasionally between these infrequent breaths, I let out an eerie and unnatural wailing scream. It seemed to them that I thought I was still trapped, and it was heart wrenching. They continued to plead with me and to pray. After what seemed like an eternity to them, I began to breathe more regularly, and time returned to "normal."

CHAPTER 12

GOING HOME

"And I am convinced that nothing can ever separate us from God's love. Neither death nor life, neither angels nor demons, Neither our fears for today nor our worries about tomorrow— Not even the powers of hell can separate us from God's love."

—Romans 8:38–39 (NLT)

∾

The current was strong and slowly pulled off my helmet and lifejacket before trying to claim my body. While still in the boat, I was seated with my legs stretched out in front of me under the front deck of the boat. I was bent forward at my waist, and my body and arms were lying on top of the front deck, pressed down by the force of the water. I was facing downstream and, as the current worked to pull my body from my boat, my body was forced to bend around the front edge of the cockpit. This was not a problem for my hips, which normally bend in that direction, but my knees were forced to fold back upon themselves in order to free my body.

It was a relatively slow process, during which I was conscious, alert, and fully aware of what was happening. It sounds rather morbid but from an orthopaedist's perspective, I was intrigued as I felt my knee bones break and my ligaments tear. I tried to analyze the sensations and consider which structures were likely involved.

I seemed to feel no pain, but wondered if I was actually screaming without knowing it. I did a quick self-assessment and decided that no, I wasn't screaming, and really wasn't feeling any pain. I felt curiously blissful. This is quite a remarkable statement considering I had always been terrified of drowning.

While my body was being slowly sucked out of the boat, I felt as though my soul was slowly peeling itself away from my body. I finally felt my body release from the boat and begin to tumble with the current. That was the last physical sensation I had with regard to my body. I do not remember scraping along the bottom of the river, bumping into Chad, or being pulled to the river bank.

At the moment my body was released and began to tumble, I felt a "pop." It felt as if I had finally shaken off my heavy outer layer, freeing my soul. I rose up and out of the river, and when my soul broke through the surface of the water, I encountered a group of fifteen to twenty souls (human spirits sent by God), who greeted me with the most overwhelming joy I have ever experienced and could ever imagine. It was joy at an unadulterated core level. They were sort of like a large welcoming committee or a great cloud of witnesses as described in **Hebrews 12:1 (ESV)**: "Therefore, since we are surrounded by so great a cloud of witnesses . . . and let us run with endurance the race that is set before us." This welcoming committee seemed to be wildly cheering for me as I approached the "finish line."

While I could not identify each spiritual being as someone by name (for instance, as Paul, my dead grandfather; Mrs. Sivits, my old babysitter; Steven, my neighbor; or other such individuals), I knew each of them well, knew they were from God, and knew that I had known them for an eternity. I was a part of them, and I knew they were sent to guide me across the divide of time and dimension that separates our world from God's. I also had the unspoken understanding that they were sent not only to greet me and guide me, but also to protect me during my journey.

They appeared as formed shapes, but not with the absolute and distinct edges of the formed physical bodies we have on earth. Their edges were blurred, as each spiritual being was dazzling and radiant. Their presence engulfed all of my senses, as though I could see, hear, feel, smell, and taste them all at once. Their brilliance was both blinding and invigorating. We did not speak, **per se,** using our mouths, but easily communicated in a very pure form. We simultaneously communicated our thoughts and emotions, and understood each other perfectly even though we did not use language.

God's word is certainly not limited to one language, and I gained a new understanding of the biblical description of Pentecost. In that story from **Acts 2:5–11 (NIV),** it is written; "Jews from every nation were staying in Jerusalem. Suddenly a sound came from heaven and the Holy Spirit began to speak. The Jews and the visitors heard declarations of the wonders of God and they were amazed, bewildered, and perplexed because each person heard the declarations in their own native language." I now understood entirely how this could be. God doesn't need verbal language for communication.

My arrival was joyously celebrated and a feeling of absolute love was palpable as these spiritual beings and I hugged, danced, and greeted each other. The intensity, depth, and purity of these feelings and sensations were far greater than I could ever describe with words and far greater than anything I have experienced on earth.

Don't get me wrong . . . I have been very blessed in my life and have experienced great joy and love here on earth. I love my husband and I love each of my children with great intensity, and that love is reciprocated. It's just that God's world is exponentially more colorful and intense. It was as though I was experiencing an explosion of love and joy in their absolute, unadulterated essence. The only earthly thing I can begin to compare this difference to is television; when you compare images on an old-style cathode-ray-tube television screen to the ones on a new high-definition television, the HD images are almost painfully crisp and clear in their relative brilliance and clarity.

Regardless, it is impossible for me to adequately describe what I saw and what I felt. When I try to recount my experiences now, the description feels very pale. I feel as though I am trying to describe a three-dimensional experience while living in a two-dimensional world. The appropriate words, descriptions, and concepts don't even exist in our current language. I have subsequently read the accounts of other people's near-death experiences and their portrayals of heaven and I am able to see the same limitations in their descriptions and vocabulary that I see in my own.

In Ned Dougherty's account of his near-death experience in the book **Fast Lane to Heaven** (Hampton Roads, 2002), he writes "Suddenly, I was enveloped in this brilliant golden light. The light was more brilliant that the light emanating from the sun, many times more powerful and radiant than the sun itself. Yet, I was not blinded by it nor was I burned by it. Instead, the light was a source of energy that embraced my being." His description, like my own, probably seems nonsensical to anyone who has not shared this type of experience, but it is really pretty accurate.

Even writers of the Bible had difficulty describing their encounters with God's angels. Matthew described his encounter with an angel of the Lord this way: "His face shown like lightning, and his clothes were white as snow" **(Matthew 28:3, NLT).** Daniel wrote: "I looked up and saw a man dressed in linen clothing, with a belt of pure gold around his waist. His body looked like a precious gem. His face flashed like lightning and his eyes flamed like torches. His arms and feet shone like polished bronze, and his voice roared like a vast multitude of people" **(Daniel 10, NLT)**.

My companions and I began to glide along a path, and I knew that I was going home. My eternal home. We were returning to God and we were all very excited. My companions could barely contain their unbridled enthusiasm and were eager to announce my return, celebrating it with all the in-habitants of heaven. As I was drinking in the beauty and rejoicing with my companions, I glimpsed back at the scene on the river bank. My body looked like the shell of a comfortable old friend, and I felt warm compassion and gratitude for its use.

I looked at Tom and his sons, and they seemed so terribly sad and vulnerable. I heard them call to me and beg me to take a breath. I loved them and did not want them to be sad, so I asked my heavenly companions to wait while I returned to my body, lay down, and took a breath. Thinking that this would be satisfactory, I then left my body and resumed my journey home.

We were traveling down a path that led to a great and brilliant hall, larger and more beautiful than anything I can conceive of seeing on earth. It was radiating a brilliance of all colors and beauty. I believe that when people with near-death experiences describe "seeing the white light" or "moving toward the white light," they may be describing their moving toward the brilliance of this hall. Our vocabulary is just not rich enough to describe the experience in a way that is understandable. Perhaps this is why Jesus often spoke in parables.

I felt my soul being pulled toward the entry and, as I approached, I physically absorbed its radiance and felt the pure, complete, and utterly unconditional absolute love that emanated from the hall. It was the most beautiful and alluring thing I had ever seen or experienced. I knew with a profound certainty that it represented the last branch point of life, the gate through which each human being must pass. It was clear that this hall is the place where each of us is given the opportunity to review our lives and our choices, and where we are each given a final opportunity to choose God or to turn away—for eternity. I felt ready to enter the hall and was filled with an intense longing to be reunited with God.

There was one notable obstacle to my reunion: Tom Long and his boys kept beckoning to me. Each time they begged me to come back and take a breath, I felt compelled to return to my body and take another breath before returning to my journey. This became tiresome, and I grew quite irritated with their repeated calling. I knew they didn't understand what was happening, but I was annoyed that they wouldn't let me go. I liken it to the irritation that a parent feels when their young child keeps asking for more things before going to bed: a story, a glass of water, the light on, the light off, the covers arranged, another kiss, and so on.

We arrived at the entrance to the hall, and I could see many spirits bustling about inside. They all turned to look at us as we began to enter, and they communicated great compassion and love. Before we could go inside, however, an oppressive feeling of grief and sadness descended upon my spiritual companions and the atmosphere became heavy. They turned to me and explained that it was not my time to enter the hall; I had not completed my journey on earth, had more work to do, and must return to my body. I protested but was given several reasons for my return and told that I would soon be given more information.

We shared our sorrow as they returned me to the river bank. I sat down in my body and gave these heavenly beings, these people who had come to guide, protect, and cheer for me, one last, longing glance before I lay down and was reunited with my body.

CHAPTER 13

ANGELS BY THE RIVER

**"Anyone who doesn't believe in miracles
Is not a realist."**

—David Ben-Gurion

૭

I became aware of my body and opened my eyes to see the faces of the Longs looking down at me. There seemed to be a sense of relief and excitement as Tom and Kenneth started telling the others what to do for me. They arranged a kayak to be my lift and secured my body to the top. The rocky river bank was adjacent to an extremely thick bamboo forest. The incline of the hillside was steep and appeared insurmountable.

As the Longs considered their options, several young Chilean men materialized out of nowhere. A couple of them helped lift and begin to carry the boat to which I was secured, and the other began to push a path through the bamboo. No words were ever spoken to them or by them; they just knew what to do. It was slow going through the forest and I faded in and out of consciousness. Kenneth has always been filled with the qualities typical of an oldest child, and his drive pushed everyone else. Despite their increasing fatigue, no one was going to stop unless he did.

During my intermittent interludes of consciousness, I would confidently blurt out instructions for them to give me steroids; I knew I couldn't move my legs and, as a spine surgeon, I assumed that I had broken my back and injured my spinal cord. If such were the case, the timely administration of steroids could lessen my degree of paralysis. This seemed like rambling to them, but it was difficult for them to ignore. Eventually they found a single-track dirt path, which led to a dirt road.

Our entourage slowly trundled along this dirt path, moving forward but not really knowing what they would do when they eventually found a road. The nearest village was too far to reach by walking and any road they came upon would be infrequently traveled. They vaguely hoped to find someone with an old tractor or other farm implement that could transport me more quickly to the village. At that time, ambulances were essentially nonexistent in this part of Chile so it was a great surprise when we emerged from the forested hillside and saw an ambulance parked on the side of the road. The driver didn't speak, but he seemed to be waiting for us.

After Bill had waved us off at the river put-in earlier in the day, he drove the truck to a sunny spot, parked and pulled out a book in preparation for a leisurely day of reading. He planned to meet us later in the day at the river take-out. During my resuscitation, one woman sort of "freaked-out" and ran away from the scene at the river. With what I am sure was God's leading, she ran to the exact spot where Bill was reading. After a quick explanation, they both jumped into the truck and rapidly drove along the road in search of our group. They found us just as I was being loaded into the ambulance.

Tom and Chad drove in the truck while Bill and Kenneth rode with me in the back of the ambulance. The driver careened down the road toward the tiny first-aid station in the village of Choshuenco, and Kenneth was somewhat reassured about my condition and my degree of comprehension when I began insisting that the driver slow down before he killed us. When we finally made it to the first-aid station, Kenneth and Chad returned to the chaos at the river. Tom stayed with Bill and me.

When Kenneth and Chad returned to the river, they first tried to find the young men who had been such a great help in carrying me through the forest. These young men were nowhere to be found and the people from the village had no idea who they could be talking about. They didn't know of anyone fitting their description in the village, so the people thought Chad and Kenneth must be mistaken. Angels? Chad and Kenneth found their return trip through the bamboo forest to the river bank was even more difficult than when they had carried me out. They found the forest to be even thicker and the hillside even steeper than they remembered. It made the success of their earlier efforts seem even less plausible, unless one accepted that the process of my rescue was almost entirely a result of divine intervention.

Once all of the remaining boaters were accounted for, Kenneth and Chad tried to recover the two boats that were still trapped at the bottom of the waterfall. It was nearly impossible. The rock upon which they had been standing when they fished me out of the water was gone. It was not possible for them to stand in the current

of the steep waterfall. It was impossible for them
to reach or even touch the boats. It took more
than an hour of dedicated working and suffering
through multiple snapped ropes to get the first
boat out. In order to achieve this, they had to first
bend and fold both boats in half by securing lines
to the boat ends and rotating them such that the
current could do this work. When they finally
retrieved the lines they had been using, they saw
that there had been enough friction and force between the lines to melt the knots together.

As they returned to Pucón, they were exhausted
and overwhelmed by the absolute impossibility
of my rescue and the supernatural aspects of what
had occurred. God's presence and purposeful intervention was clear to all those who were present
on the scene. Tom, Kenneth, Chad, and Anne
have all told me they feel that the situation went
from one of total and absolute failure and hopelessness to one of success without any meaningful
input from them. They have described it to me as
a choreographed performance in which they were
each just playing their roles. To this day, they
continue to feel that ours is not just a good story.
It wasn't just one miracle; it was a constellation of
miracles for which there is no possible explanation other than God's intervention. As Chad later
said, "Let's not let life muddle what happened.
We were all part of a miracle."

Anne has reported that she was overwhelmed by the simultaneous and contrasting feelings of being so helpless and small in the universe and of being so loved by God that He chose to be present. She, and I think all of us, are still feeling undeserving of His intervention. With all of the suffering and people in need, it is difficult to understand how or why He intervened that day on the Fuy River in Chile, but He clearly did.

Anne has described feeling both helpless and remarkably liberated. She knows that God is in control and she feels that she now understands the verse in the Bible that describes how you must give up everything in order to gain everything:

> **"For those who want to save their life will lose it, and those who lose their life for my sake, and for the sake of the gospel, will save it."**
>
> **—Mark 8:35 (NRS)**

CHAPTER 14

RETURN TO WYOMING

"I will never leave you nor forsake you."

—Hebrews 13:5 (NKJV)

∽

The first-aid clinic in Choshuenco was quite rudimentary, with no diagnostic equipment and few supplies. Bill was relieved to find a supply of plaster however, and expertly applied long splints to each of my legs. I don't think I said much, as I felt myself drifting back and forth between this world and the one I had left. I was still fully immersed in the visions, the passion, the intensity, and the love I had just witnessed in God's kingdom.

In trying to sort out and make sense of what was happening, I made one absolute decision: I was not going to stay in Chile for my medical care, nor was I going to stop in any of the large American cities through which we would pass on our way back to our home in Wyoming. Jackson Hole had a great hospital, doctors that I trusted and, most importantly, I knew that I needed to be with my children.

Bill and Tom loaded me into the backseat of the pickup truck for the beginning of our journey home. We drove to Coique, where there was a small airport. Finding the airport closed, we drove on to Valdivia, a bustling city of more than 100,000. Bill's heart sank and he was brought to tears as we approached the airport entrance and saw that the entry gate was closed and locked. There would be no more flights until the morning.

We drove into the city and found a small hotel with a vacancy. As Tom said goodbye, Bill carried me up the stairs and we settled in for a long and restless night of waiting for the morning. A taxi returned us to the airport at the crack of dawn, at which point Bill found a small plane that was going to Santiago. He secured seats and gently lifted me into the plane. Bill was heroic. He dealt with the bags, the tickets, and with me in my debilitated condition.

I cannot tell you why we decided to take commercial flights rather than calling for a medical evacuation, but it seemed like the right thing to do. Bill carried me off one plane and onto the next. The flight from Santiago to Dallas carried few people, and there were several empty seats across which I could stretch out. Although the flight attendants raised their eyebrows at my appearance and behavior, none questioned my condition too thoroughly.

We were met with a wheelchair upon our arrival at Dallas/Fort Worth International Airport and we uneventfully passed through customs and back into the United States. Bill thought it would attract less interest if only one of my legs was bundled up, so prior to boarding our next flight to Salt Lake City, Utah, he removed the splint from one of my legs. Despite this, the flight attendants expressed significant concern after watching Bill gently lift me into my seat. In response to their questions, we stretched the truth . . . a lot. We explained that we were both orthopaedic surgeons and that I had injured my ankle while on vacation and we simply thought I would be more comfortable with it splinted.

The flight attendants clearly did not believe this fable, so they brought the flight's captain to speak with us. He explained his concern that I would be a hindrance and an obstacle in the event of an emergency landing or crash. I chuckled internally and wanted to explain that after what I had already been through, I was sure this would be the safest flight he had ever flown. What I actually said was that I was trained in emergency situations, my injury really wasn't too bad, and I would definitely not slow anyone down. Satisfied, he returned to the cockpit, and we were on our way.

I began to have some difficulty breathing upon our arrival in Utah. When we stopped for something to drink, I found that I was weak, ill, and unable to breathe deeply or fully. I felt very distant and I don't think either Bill or I were thinking clearly at this point. We never discussed going to one of the local hospitals in Salt Lake City, as I was resolute in returning to Jackson for my care. Thinking that I might have a blood clot or pneumonia, we telephoned my internist and asked him to meet us in our office upon our return.

Bill then loaded me into the backseat of our pickup truck, and we started the five-hour drive from Utah to our home in Wyoming. When my breathing became even more labored several hours into the drive, I began to question my decisions and to wonder if I would make it back to my children. Bill called my internist and suggested that he should meet us in the emergency room rather than in our own medical facility.

The elevation gain as we drove over Pine Creek Pass (elevation 6,720 feet) caused my breathing to deteriorate even further. I began to apologize to my husband—my loving, faithful, constant husband whom I adored. He had been one of God's greatest gifts to me, and I apologized to him for not being able to make it home, for not stopping sooner, for choosing to return to Jackson, for leaving him, for dying. I apologized again and again and again.

In Chile I had felt confident about my decision to return to Jackson Hole because I thought it was God's plan. Now that it looked like I would die before reaching home, I was filled with remorse at my presumed misunderstanding. I was overcome with grief for my husband and for my young children. Willie, Betsy, Eliot, and Peter were so loving and vulnerable that I felt great sorrow at not being able to make it for them . . . for failing them.

CHAPTER 15

THE POWER OF PRAYER

"If two of you on earth agree about
anything you ask for, It will be done
for you by my Father in heaven.
For where two or three come
together in my name,
There am I with them."

—Matthew 18:19–20 (NIV)

༁

As we drove over Teton Pass (elevation 8,431
feet), I began breathing so shallowly and taking
in so little oxygen that I could no longer speak.
Although I was quite comfortable, I began to
fade in and out of consciousness as my usually
law-abiding husband pushed harder on the ac-
celerator and forced the speedometer ever higher.
When we reached the hospital parking lot, the
truck door was jerked open and I was quickly
moved out of the truck and onto a gurney by the
emergency room staff.

When I looked up from the gurney and recognized the face of my internist looking down at
me, I knew I was at last home and immediately
lost consciousness. I was taken into the emergency
room and placed in one of the small examination cubicles. My oxygen levels were dangerously
low and did not respond to the administration of
oxygen.

Preliminary evaluation showed an advanced
pneumonia and acute respiratory distress syndrome (ARDS). ARDS is a severe inflammatory
reaction in the lungs to a major insult, such as a
near drowning, fat embolism, pneumonia, smoke
inhalation, or other major trauma. This reactive
swelling of the lung tissue often develops after
twenty-four to forty-eight hours, interferes with
the ability to exchange oxygen, and often leads to
death. My internist gravely told my husband that
I would probably not make it through the night.

Natalie, the medical assistant of my internist,
was sitting in the cubicle next to mine, separated
by a thin curtain. She had driven another member of our church, Sherry, to the emergency room
for the treatment of a cut finger. When they saw
the facial expressions of the people around me
and heard the words of my internist, they immediately began to pray. They prayed for the saving
of my life, for the healing of my body, for the

emotional strength of my family, and for us to be enveloped by God's grace. They prayed intensely, passionately, and specifically. They soon left the emergency room and went to the high school basketball game, where much of the community was cheering on our young people. They quickly sent around the message of my injury and encouraged others to begin praying. Within an hour of my emergency room arrival, there were a great many people praying for me. Natalie went home and continued to pray fervently. She prayed until four in the morning, when suddenly she felt like she could rest.

While others were lifting me up to the Lord with their prayers, I was lying in the intensive care unit. For much of the night, my body struggled for survival. According to the medical records, about 4 A.M., the same time Natalie felt released from prayer, my vital signs stabilized and the nurses were able to take a tentative sigh of relief. It looked like I was going to make it after all.

A friend of mine later told me that she thought I survived the night because with all of those people praying for me, God would have been embarrassed to let me die. I don't know about that, but God's compassion certainly reinforced the power of prayer to everyone involved.

CHAPTER 16

CLARITY OF VISION

"Don't worry about anything;
Instead, pray about everything.
Tell God what you need,
And thank him for all he has done.
If you do this,
You will experience God's peace."

—Philippians 4:6 (NLT)

∽

I was awakened the following morning by the arrival of two deacons from our church. They own a local outdoor shop and came bearing a stack of great magazines for me to read. As delightful as my deacons were, I will admit that I was looking forward to their departure so I could get started on the magazines. Strangely, I felt great. I had no pain and was quite clear mentally.

I picked up a **Cross Country Skier** magazine as soon as they left and was surprised to find that, despite my historically having 20/20 vision, the pages were too blurry for me to read. I put them aside and turned on the television. The picture on the screen was too blurry for me to understand. The nurse came in and I found that she, too, looked blurry. I was no longer comfortable having a conversation, as I could not look at any one spot for more than a couple of seconds without the blurriness becoming too uncomfortable. It was very distracting and irritating, so I opted to take a nap. When I awoke, I asked the nurse if there was a Bible anywhere. She produced a Gideon's Bible—I always wondered who read those—and I proceeded to look for verses about gaining strength and such. I looked to **Psalms** and searched for well-known verses such as these:

"God is our refuge and strength, an ever-present help in trouble."

—Psalm 46:1 (NIV)

"When you call to me, I will answer you. I will be with you when you are in trouble. I will save you and honor you."

—Psalm 91:15 (God's Word)

"I can do all things through him who strengthens me."

—Philippians 4:13 (NRS)

Unfortunately, the printing in the Bible was also too blurry for me to read. Just as I was closing the book in frustration and tossing it aside, something distinct and clear flashed before my eyes. Presuming that my vision had cleared, I returned to the psalms. The words were still blurry. Again I began to carelessly flip through the pages as I closed the book. Again, something became clear and legible. I then carefully searched through the pages until I was able to find the verse that was crystal clear . . .

It read:

"Rejoice always."

—1 Thessalonians 5:16 (ESV)

Wow. I began to contemplate the meaning of this verse, as it was clearly a directive from God. In my contemplations, I thought about the fact that a joyful heart and a joyful spirit are clearly important to God, and the word "joy" is mentioned throughout all the books of the Bible. I had always been a "happy" person and generally saw the rosy side of things, but joy is clearly different than happiness. It is not based on circumstances, but on the presence, hope, and promises of God. Even when it feels as if we are being crushed by earthly troubles, we can remain joyful. If we keep our focus on God, our spirit cannot be trampled. Joy is a state of mind and a state of being. It reflects a conscious choice to believe in the promises of the Bible.

Later in the day, a second verse became clear to my vision. It read:

"Pray without ceasing."

—1 Thessalonians 5:17 (ESV)

Prayer is the way we are able to communicate with our Lord. This verse directs us to maintain a continually open line of communication with Him. It instructs us that we should live a life of prayer, continuously offering silent prayers with every breath we take, and always listening for God's leading.

In the past, I had believed in the power to pray for one's self: for forgiveness, for change, for insight, and so forth. I had subscribed to the concept that prayer does not change the outcome of a situation, but it changes us in the process. While I still hold firmly to my belief in this aspect of prayer, I have subsequently realized that it does not represent the whole story, for Jesus said, "Where two or three are gathered in my name, I am there among them." I had now personally experienced this promise of Jesus and the remarkable power of people praying for the well-being of others. I began to see my life and each breath I am given as a living prayer to God and a way to pray for others and for our world.

The last verse that became clear to my vision that day was this:

"Give thanks in all circumstances, for this is the will of God's in Christ Jesus for you."

—1 Thessalonians 5:18 (ESV)

Double and triple wow! I was immediately reminded of the often-told fable about giving thanks and being grateful for little things:

"When a poor man was given a loaf of bread, he thanked the baker, but the baker said, 'Don't thank me. Thank the miller who made the flour.' So the poor man thanked the miller, but the miller said, 'Don't thank me. Thank the farmer who planted the wheat.' So the poor man thanked the farmer. But the farmer said, 'Don't thank me. Thank the Lord. He gave the sunshine and rain and fertility to the soil, and that's why you have bread to eat.'"

The rest of the Bible, other written material, the television, and even the faces of those people I love continued to be blurry for several days. Due to this continued blurriness, I wasn't able to read anything other than these three Bible verses, couldn't watch TV, and didn't want to converse with anyone. All I did was read and re-read these three verses. These are three of the briefest verses in the Bible, yet I believe they are far reaching and summarize much of what God asks of us.

CHAPTER 17

CONVERSING WITH AN ANGEL

**"Ask and you will receive;
Seek and you will find;
Knock and the door will be opened to you."**

—Matthew 7:7 (GNT)

∽

I spent a great number of hours contemplating what God was asking of me. Even before my boating accident, I did not really believe in luck or coincidence as phenomena. I believed that God has a hand in most things and that most of what happens is part of a larger plan. I was laying in my hospital bed wondering about the purpose of my accident when I suddenly found myself sitting on a rock in a large, sun-drenched field.

I was having a "conversation" with an angel who was sitting on a nearby rock. I call the being an angel, but I don't really know what he was: angel, messenger, Christ, or teacher. I do know that he was of God, in God, and from God. As we conversed, I asked questions, and he gave me answers. We discussed how to "rejoice always," even in the midst of terrible circumstances, and discussed the longstanding question, "Why do bad things happen to good people?" During this conversation, I received the following wisdom.

We are each given the opportunity and privilege to come to earth for different reasons. Sometimes we come in order that we may personally develop and strengthen the fruits of our spirit: those of love, kindness, patience, joy, peace, goodness, faithfulness, gentleness, and self-control. Sometimes we come to help someone else develop the fruits of the spirit. We all come to earth to become more Christ-like, as noted in **Romans 8.**

In preparation for our journey to earth, we are able to make a basic outline for our life. This is not to imply that we, the humans, are entirely in charge of our life's design. It is more like God creates it, then we review it and discuss it with our "personal planning" angel. Within the algorithm are written branch points in our lives at which times we may exit, returning to God, or we may be redirected to a different task and goal.

We may be directed to these branch points by our own conscious choice and by our circumstances, or we may be pushed along by angelic intervention. Have you ever shown up somewhere at "just the right time"? When you think back on your life, can you remember a person who briefly entered your life, saying something or doing something that impacted your life out of proportion to what they actually said or did? What were the circumstances that brought you together with your spouse or the detailed circumstances of other such notable events in your life? Have you ever been randomly thinking of someone who then unexpectedly shows up or contacts you? Has something ever happened that left you thinking "That's weird"? Consider whether these are sets of "coincidences" or whether they might be orchestrated events; evidence of God's hand in our lives.

Although we are rarely aware of angels or their intervention in our world, I believe there are angels all around us every day of our lives. Angels are spirit beings who are mentioned more than 250 times in both the Old Testament and the New Testament of the Bible. They appear as creatures, events, and humans, offering praise and worship to God. They care for, protect, and guide God's people, frequently intervening or bringing messages to people from God. They are the ones orchestrating the "coincidences" that occur so commonly in our lives.

Of note is that most theologians would agree that angels live among us according to God's will, not our own. Lewis Sperry Chafer wrote in **Systematic Theology** (Kregel, 1993), "One reason angels are rendered invisible to human sight may be that if they were seen, they would be worshiped. Man, who is so prone to idolatry as to worship the works of his own hands, would hardly be able to resist the worship of angels were they before his eyes."

While often unrecognized, angels certainly seem to be present and active in our world today. A **Newsweek** article titled "In Search of the Sacred" (November 1994) observed, "Twenty percent of Americans have had a revelation from God in the last year, and 13 percent have seen or sensed the presence of an angel."

Angels often expose us to, or push us into, a situation that will force our redirection. Of course, our redirection is not **really** forced; rather, as we are compelled to approach the fork in our road, we make a choice to turn left or turn right. Every choice leads us forward, and there is no going backward, no "redo." Every choice we make today affects the choices that we face tomorrow. Planet earth and the humans living on it are truly interconnected, and there is no action without some sort of reaction.

Even the most terrible circumstances and events can stimulate great change in individuals and/or societies. Without observing cruelty, we would not be moved to compassion. Without personal trials, we would not develop patience or faithfulness. It is the recognition that our earthly concerns matter little when compared to life eternal that allows us to know joy in the midst of sorrow and worry. Have you ever really changed or experienced personal growth during times of comfort or complacency? The acceptance that change rarely comes without difficulty and challenge can truly free a person to "rejoice always." It also allows us to live daily with a grateful heart and "give thanks in all circumstances." No matter what the circumstances, we can be grateful that God fulfills His promises, that our faith is sufficient to sustain us, and that our eternal life is assured.

Sometimes uncomfortable situations or irritating people are placed in our lives to lead us in a direction more in line with God's will. One example I like to use is that of a beggar who may sit outside of a wealthy businessman's office in an attempt to help that person develop more tolerance and compassion for others.

I am able to see examples of this in my own life as well. Before my accident, the behavior of some of my colleagues deeply aggravated and irritated me. Afterward, while I still didn't like the behavior, I realized that I do not know their purpose on earth, nor why they are in my life. As difficult as it sometimes is to accept, I do know that God loves each of them every bit as much as He loves me. Rather than being irritated by their behavior, I now take joy in the knowledge that their behavior is teaching me patience and I give thanks for this. I also began to pray for them, which has changed my perspective significantly. The exercise of praying for others (and I'm talking about praying with love, not praying as is humorously presented in the country-western song about praying for the car brakes to go out, the flower pot to fall, the engine to stall, and such) can lead to dramatic results and to greater peace and contentment. This exercise is definitely worth trying.

As the angel sitting on the nearby rock continued his explanations and patiently answered my questions, I began to visualize a reasonable analogy for our individual lives; each of us is like a small piece of thread that contributes to the weaving of a very large and very beautiful tapestry. We, as single threads, spend our lives worrying about our thread—what color it is and how long it is—even becoming upset if it becomes torn or frayed. The complete tapestry is far too large for us to see and of too complex a pattern for us to appreciate the importance of our single thread. Regardless, without our individual contribution, the tapestry would be incomplete and broken. We should, therefore, recognize and take joy in our contribution. Indeed, our threads— our lives—are important; what we do and the choices we make, even the seemingly small ones, actually make a difference.

I find it interesting that when people describe how terribly awful some events or circumstances are, it is rarely the people directly involved who are doing this describing. I have spoken to person after person who has been at the center of a situation described by others as "awful, tragic, or disastrous," yet they themselves are grateful for the situation and would not change their circumstances if they were given the choice.

My point is this: interpreting something that happens as being inherently "good" or "bad" is entirely a matter of perspective. Do "bad things happen to good people"? I'm not so sure. Jesus was certainly a very "good" man. His crucifixion would certainly be interpreted by many as a "bad" thing. His disciples were devastated, yet the Old Testament prophecies would not have been fulfilled and a new covenant with God would not exist if Jesus had not been crucified. From this perspective, it is difficult to declare that the crucifixion of Jesus was a "bad" thing. In fact, it is the very heart of the "good news" that Christians celebrate.

Even when we are frustrated by our inability to understand a circumstance or event, there are unseen angels bringing comfort and protection as directed by the wisdom of God. Our only reasonable option is to rely on the word and promises of God.

CHAPTER 18

THE PATIENT CARE UNIT

**"This is the day the Lord has made;
Let us rejoice
And Be glad in it."**

—Psalm 118:24 (NIV)

∾

When my health allowed for it, I was transferred to the patient care unit (PCU). When I first arrived, I still had no pain to speak of and still felt wrapped in the cloak of God. I actually felt blissful. When people entered my room for the first time, they would literally take a step backward and with a look of surprise on their faces ask, "What is going on in here?" They would go on to describe a feeling of physical power and presence in the room. The first time someone noted this, I sort of ignored it. When it occurred again and again, and with a variety of different people, I began to believe that they were feeling the almost palpable energy in my room. I should not have been surprised that they could feel God's presence—I could certainly feel it.

It had been a couple of weeks since my accident, but I was still spending most of each day in pensive contemplation, trying to make sense of all that had happened. I believed that all things work together for good and I began to contemplate the possible reasons for this accident. Before I knew it, I was once again sitting in a beautiful, sun-drenched field with an angel. The brilliance and intensity of the surrounding beauty and the purity of the angel's radiant love were simultaneously overwhelming and rejuvenating.

We spoke for what seemed like many hours, and I never wanted to leave. We talked about the specifics of my accident and I was given more information regarding many of the reasons I was returned to earth. Later in this book, I will tell you about several of these directives, including the protection of my husband's health, being a rock of support for my family and community after the death of my son, helping others find their way back to God, and sharing my story and experiences.

When our conversation was over and it was time for me to return, the angel kissed me on my forehead and bade me farewell. I knew it would

be our last conversation and with that kiss, much
of what had been told to me seemed to be placed
beneath a veil. I sensed that I could later choose
to lift the veil and recall all of the words said to
me if I really wanted to, but I also knew that I
was expected to let them remain veiled.

With my transfer to the PCU came the added
joy of being allowed visitors. I looked forward to
my children's first visit and ached with a longing to
hold each of them tightly and reassuringly. When
they arrived, my three older kids were reluctant
to approach me and my youngest stayed as far
away from my bed as was possible. I imagine that
I must have been frightening to see, and perhaps
unrecognizable with all of the various tubes and
machinery attached to my body, but their hesita-
tion was heartbreaking. Within a few days, their
comfort was restored and we spent glorious hours
lying together in my hospital bed watching movies and cuddling. Although I adored them and
loved the time we spent together, part of me still
longed to be with God. This realization made me
feel torn and depressed.

One afternoon I was awakened by a visit from
Al Forbes, one of the partners in my medical practice. He was a Christian man and I felt I could
tell him the details of my extraordinary experiences on the river. As I told him of my drowning,

of God's loving embrace, and of the miracles that had occurred, he began to cry. I asked why he was crying and was surprised when he told me that he was overcome with envy at my being so close to God, and was crying because he was not usually an envious man. Not wanting to upset others, I then chose not to tell many more people the details or extent of my experiences with God.

As my physical state became one of recovery rather than survival, I was more fully absorbed back into the reality of this world. My ties with God's world became less palpable until I was no longer able to pass between worlds or have conversations with angels. When my medical condition improved and my orthopaedic partners (including my husband) were able to agree upon a treatment plan, I was finally able to undergo the first of several operations to surgically repair my various injuries. With this beginning of physical recovery, I also began to feel pain.

The rest of my time in the hospital was challenging for everyone. I was still trying to process all that I had witnessed and continued to meditate on the three verses from **1 Thessalonians,** but both of my legs were in casts stretching from my toes to my hips so I was unable to move and was able to do very little. Bill was at work during the day, the older kids were in school, and Peter was with our nanny, Kasandra. Since I was on my back with only the ceiling for my entertainment, I counted the small holes in each ceiling tile again and again; first vertically, then horizontally, then diagonally. The excitement of coming up with the same number each time did little to diminish my boredom.

Visitors were exhausting but served as bright interludes to this otherwise dreary time. One friend rolled my bed into the sunshine that was delightfully streaming through a hallway window, and one thoughtful friend brought me some lavender body lotion that smelled like a field of fresh blossoms. Each time I rubbed some of this lotion on my hands I would delight in its scent and be enveloped in a feeling of comfort and beauty. It meant so much to me at the time that I have saved the bottle. Now when I occasionally open it and inhale the remnants of its fragrance, I am immediately reminded of my feeling of delight and fondly remember the person who gave it to me.

After more than a month in the hospital, I was not sorry to pack up my belongings and go home.

CHAPTER 19

MY PHYSICAL RECOVERY

**"Life isn't about waiting for
the showers to pass.
It's about learning to dance in the rain."**

—Vivian Greene

∽

I was excited to leave the hospital, but once I was home I was emotionally depressed and physically miserable. Yes, I found joy in my circumstances, but that did not change my tangible, daily, physical reality. I had solid casts on both legs, which extended from my groin to my toes. I wasn't able to move around by myself, although I could stand upright on my own with a walker if someone first lifted me up. If no one was nearby to assist me, I was wheelchair-bound.

Our rental house was probably built in the 1970s, with very narrow doors and hallways. A friend removed the doors from the hinges so I could be wheeled between my bedroom and the kitchen, but I was basically like a pet rock. After someone moved me into a room, I had to stay there until someone arrived to move me into a different location.

While still in the hospital, I had developed blood clots in my legs that broke free and traveled to my lungs. To help dissolve the blood clots and avoid further complications, Bill gave me twice daily shots—not a pleasant experience for someone who detests being stuck with a needle. I was also taking narcotic pills for the pain and required help for even the most basic activities of daily living. The euphoria of visiting heaven was gone, replaced by the tedium of each day and the continued disbelief that I had been sent back to earth. I was really quite glum. I had always been physically active and strong, and being physically immobile was emotionally difficult for me. It was challenging to follow the disciple James's dictum: "Consider it all joy . . . when you face trials of many kinds because you know that the testing of your faith develops perseverance." I thought I had developed enough perseverance.

Scott was one of the nurse's aides at the hospital with whom Bill contracted to provide home health care to me a couple of times weekly. He was strong, nurturing, and always cheerful. I looked forward to these visits and relished the joyful energy he provided. He would move me from room to room, wash my hair, make my lunch, find the sunshine, and just sit with me. Despite these visits, I was languishing. Some of my more creative friends decided to take action; they attached two skis to the bottom of a snowmobile sled and built a seat inside the sled. They then attached a handle to the back of the sled, making it possible for Scott to load me into the sled and push me along the snow-covered street outside my house . . . I was thus capable of being taken for a walk like a baby in a pram!

Sometimes I would be pushed slowly, but sometimes Scott would take me to one of the nearby hills and let me work up some speed in the sled while he ran behind. I began to take some short ski poles with me on these outings and I became fairly competent at sitting in the sled while jubilantly steering it by digging the poles into the snow on one side or the other. Traveling in the sled was the only time I felt mobile, so it was magnificent. When I was in the sled, I felt alive. My family began to call Scott "Sleigh Boy," since all I wanted to do when he arrived was to load up the sleigh and have him take me out. Scott was so helpful in my recovery that I was a little sorry to say goodbye when I became strong enough and mobile enough to finally care for myself. He has since left our town and become a physician's assistant. I have not heard from him in many years, but I recall him fondly and will always cherish the kindness he showed to me.

My youngest son, Peter, was only 1 ½ years old when I had my kayaking accident. He had been the most hesitant to be near me while I was in the hospital, but he never left my side once I returned home. For many months, his love, constancy, comfort, and a shared knowledge of God's presence kept me linked to him and, through him, to this world. Given his very young age, I believe he still remembered God's world, which seemed to give him an understanding of the spiritual aspect of my experience and what I was going through. My older children were great sources of joy, reassurance, and inspiration, and Kasandra, our wonderful nanny, provided a great sense of stability to all of us.

Although I was physically present in our home, I was emotionally absent. I was quite absorbed into my own world of physical recovery and emotional turmoil as I tried to process all that had happened to me. It took me more than a year to finally accept that not only had I been sent back to earth, but that I had work left to do. I was part of a family that I dearly loved, and I finally accepted that I better get on with my life and make the most of it. During this time, Bill was the glue that held our lives together. He worked full-time in his own orthopaedic practice, maintained my orthopaedic practice, cared for our children, changed Peter's diapers, made sure everyone was fed, administered my shots, and organized my medical treatment, all while trying to process his own feelings of helplessness and grief about what had happened. Despite being emotionally and physically drained, he was exceptional.

The community in which we live was also so supportive of our family that it can make me cry even now to think about it. Someone from our church or elsewhere in our community brought food to our house every night for many months. Occasionally, people would spend their weekend "holding down our fort" so that Bill could go skiing or do something else for himself. We had not lived in our community for very long before my accident so didn't even know most of these people, and many of them did not know us. But they embraced our need nonetheless and their kindness to us was a tremendous blessing.

Betsy, Peter, Willie, and Eliot just before our move
to Jackson Hole, Wyoming

Years later, my oldest son, Willie, on his
way to climb the Grand Teton.

**Bill and I relaxing in the Chilean sun
before driving to the river.**

**Bill and I are at the put-in for my run down the
upper section of the Fuy. I am wearing his bright
red paddling jacket.**

Looking down on a section of the Fuy River. This beautiful river is made inaccessible by it rocky banks and steep, thickly forested hillsides.

I was pinned beneath the turbulence at the bottom of the drop to this kayaker's left.

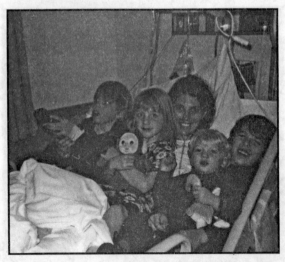

Once I was medically stable, Willie, Betsy, Peter, Eliot, and I snuggled and watched movies from my hospital bed.

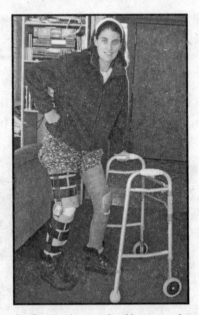

Walking was definitely a challenge, but it was a joy to be upright and somewhat mobile after being in a wheelchair for so long.

I, Peter, Willie, Bill, Betsy, and Eliot.
This Easter 2004 family vacation changed
the course of our lives.

October 2010; Betsy, Mary, Peter, Eliot and Bill on
our first trip without Willie

**I love the water and still enjoy
kayaking whenever possible.**

**I continue to find satisfaction as a surgeon,
although I now try to integrate the spiritual
component of healing.**

Willie posts his first "No Idling" sign in Jackson Hole. Since then, his message of making a difference has continued to inspire people, a growing number of Idle-reduction campaigns have been championed, and signs have been posted in at least thirty cities.

CHAPTER 20

BOB

**"I have fought the good fight,
I have finished the race,
I have kept the faith."**

—2 Timothy 4:7 (NKJV)

∾

Two weeks after my discharge from the hospital, I received a phone call telling me that my father, Bob, was being taken off life-support. What??? Though my brain was working well and I could hear the words, I could not understand the information I was being given. I hadn't even known my father was in the hospital, so how could I possibly understand that his life-sustaining ventilator was being removed?

As the story unfolded, I discovered that two weeks earlier he wasn't feeling well when he had had been visiting my brother in San Francisco. Upon his return to Michigan, he developed severe pneumonia. My father was admitted to the hospital for treatment, but when his condition did not improve with antibiotics, he was placed on a ventilator in an attempt to improve his oxygen transfer. His condition continued to worsen despite this aggressive care and, when his internal organs sequentially failed, my stepmother made the decision to remove his external life support. Inexplicably, she had also made the decision not to contact me or any of my three siblings (we were all children from his previous marriage) when he was hospitalized, when his conditioned worsened, or before she made the final decision of removing his external life support.

Over the years, my father's relationship with my siblings and me had been strained by the circumstances in which he lived. He often spoke of how he desperately wanted a close relationship with each of us, but that his wife was entirely unsupportive of this and presented many obstacles. She was a widow with five children, several of whom still lived at home with her and my father. I just don't think she wanted to accept the fact that my father had a life prior to their marriage or that he had four grown children of his own. She prevented him from having our photographs in their house, calling us from their home, or going out of his way to visit us. He cried often when discussing this with us, but was unable, or un-

willing, to demand change. My father's impend-
ing death would make the strained relationships
final and abolish any possibility of reconciliation.
For these reasons, I knew the importance of our
seeing our father before his last thread of connection to life was severed.

Without speaking to my stepmother, I contacted my father's attending physician and pleaded
with him to maintain the life support until my
siblings and I could arrive. Although this would
require my father to be on the ventilator an extra
day or two, as we were each coming from distant
parts of the country, he very grudgingly agreed
to do so. I am chagrined to admit that his agreement came only after I acted like a bully.

My siblings were at the airport when I arrived
and we drove directly to my father's hospital.
When I entered the room where my father was
lying in his hospital bed, I saw that he was se-
dated and the ventilator was rhythmically pushing air in and out of his lungs. Although he was
still "alive," I had the overwhelming sense, really
more of a deep knowledge, that his soul had already departed from his body. He was already
dead. Although it is a commonly-held belief that
a person's soul departs at the moment of their
physical death, I have come to believe that the
departure of the soul defines and determines the

moment of death, rather than the body's physical death determining the moment of the soul's departure. With the use of modern medicine and technology, the organism that is our human body may continue to physically function and appear to be "alive," but unless God sees a purpose to return the soul to its body, the person is essentially dead. Not only had I witnessed this during my surgical training, but there are far too many accounts of near-death experiences in which there is a description of the soul departing the shell of its not-yet physically dead body to ignore this reality.

My father had been a vivacious, active, and physically fit man. He and his twin brother had been National Collegiate Athletic Association track stars, part of an elite crowd of champions and members of the NCAA Hall of Fame. My emotions were mixed as I had a chance to sit alone in the hospital room with my father's now pale and somewhat shrunken body. I felt joy for him—for his reunion with God—and I felt a little bit sorry for myself, as I still had not reconciled the need for my own return to earth from the river bank in Chile. I regretted that I did not have a final opportunity to express my love and gratitude to Dad for his life, and even more deeply saddened that I never had the opportunity to tell him of my recent experiences in heaven. I could have given him a glimpse of the great joy awaiting his arrival and I think that hearing about it would have made his departure more tranquil.

My brothers, Rob and Bill, my sister, Betsy, our stepmother, and I were at my father's bedside when the ventilator tube was removed from his body and he slowly took his last breath.

Afterward, Rob, Bill, Betsy, and I returned to our hotel room, where we reminisced, cried, and laughed long into the night as each of us recalled our childhood adventures with our father. We spent the next several days organizing the flowers and programs, while our stepmother tended to other aspects of his memorial service. To be fair, I should say that my siblings did the organizing while I waited in the car or wherever else they put me since both of my legs were still immobilized in long casts and it was a slow struggle for me to follow them with my walker.

I already described the First Presbyterian Church in Kalamazoo, Michigan, as being elegant, old, and beautiful. During my father's funeral, the large, traditional stained glass windows bathed the main sanctuary with an array of color.

As I sank into the familiar front row pew, I allowed my mind to go backward in time to embrace and re-experience the wonder I always felt as a child when looking at the images in those same windows.

My father had been well known and well respected in our state, and it seemed that everyone in the region had turned out to pay their last respects. It was a long service, but the attendees were patient as I was painstakingly helped to rise from my wheelchair and step up to the podium to deliver one of his eulogies. By the time the bagpipes played "Amazing Grace" at the end of the service, I was thoroughly exhausted.

My trip back to Wyoming required a change of planes in Cincinnati, Ohio. My flight to Salt Lake City was just beginning to board when the fire alarm in the terminal sounded. Despite having traveled extensively, I never had this experience and will probably never encounter it again! Everyone in the terminal was instructed to exit the building and stand outside on the tarmac. I tried to follow these instructions but had no one to help me as I rolled myself along with the crowd. I was soon stranded in my wheelchair at the top of a very long stairway leading to the tarmac and, as the other people streamed outside, I began to cry in frustration.

I was feeling extremely sorry for myself and my situation. There were no airport employees anywhere in sight and, thinking that it was more important for Bill to stay in Wyoming with our children, I had declined Bill's offer to travel with me to Michigan. I just couldn't believe that after all I'd been through I was going to die in a fire. I didn't even have a working cell phone to call for help or to phone in my last goodbyes! After a while, an airport employee saw me and, when I explained my predicament, told me, "Don't worry about it. It's just a false alarm anyway."

Okay. God still had plans for me.

CHAPTER 21

MY BELOVED GEORGE

**"You will find as you look back upon
your life that the moments when you
have really lived, are the moments when you
have done things in a spirit of love."**

—Henry Drummond

∽

After my return from Michigan, my mother arrived in Jackson Hole to help care for me and to
help my husband care for our children. The day
after her arrival, we discovered that my stepfather, like my father several weeks earlier, had just
been admitted to his local hospital with a case
of pneumonia. This was not George's first bout
of pneumonia, as he had a form of myelodys-
plasia, which is a blood disorder that frequently
results in pneumonia. Remarkably, my father's
pneumonia was caused by a similar blood disorder; something he had been living with but had
kept secret until his final hospitalization. I spoke

with George's physician, who reassured me that my stepfather appeared to be responding well to the antibiotics, so we should not be overly concerned.

Despite this reassurance, my mother and I considered whether or not she should return to North Carolina to be with George. As we pondered this issue over our morning coffee, a great grey owl swooped down and landed on the deck railing adjacent to our breakfast area. Having never seen this type of owl, we were awed and stood to admire it.

They are large and elegant animals. We saw that one of our cats was also on the deck and wondered how the two animals would react to each other. Our cat slowly walked to the railing and reached up toward the owl. The owl, which could easily have eaten it for a snack, gave our cat a quick look, disregarded it, and continued to stare in our direction. The owl seemed to have concern only for us.

Throughout that day and subsequent days, the owl appeared to follow us as we moved from room to room. My stepfather and I continued to have a loving disagreement over the telephone about which of us needed my mother's help more—he said **me,** and I said **him**—until by the week's end, I was determined to send my mother home. As my mother was climbing into the taxi to begin her trip home, the great grey owl settled onto a nearby post and simply stared at me insistently, as it had done all week. I could not ignore the intensity of its gaze and felt as though it would come and land directly on my head if I didn't immediately give it my full attention. The bird clearly had something to say and, when I finally paid attention, I felt the owl urging me to go with my mother to North Carolina.

My stepfather and I had an extremely close and important bond. If George were to die without my being present, I knew I would be devastated and overcome with remorse. Despite my continued disability and the difficulty of traveling in my condition, I decided to accompany my mother. I grabbed my purse, gave one last look of gratitude to the owl for its guidance and persistence, and tried to scramble into the taxi.

The trip to North Carolina was ambitious and arduous. We had rushed to the Jackson Hole airport, but just missed the last flight for the day. A friend graciously drove us five hours to the Salt Lake City airport, but spending the night in the backseat of his pickup truck while we waited for the next flight was not very restful, to say the least!

When we finally arrived at the side of my step-father's hospital bed, we found him to be in good spirits. George's son, Larry, was also present, and we had some wonderful and loving conversations. We all celebrated my mother's birthday in George's hospital room the next day. George laughed, felt great, and was even able to eat a bit of his favorite food: cookies.

My mom and I were quite relieved at his condition and were in high spirits the next morning. We sat at her breakfast table sipping coffee and contemplating George's health and the possibility of his release from the hospital. As we chatted, we looked out the picture window and gazed upon a large, entirely barren Bradford pear tree. My mother then told me the story of that tree.

She and George loved the large, pink blossoms of the many Bradford pear trees in their neighborhood, so they had planted this tree many years prior with the hope of enjoying its annual display of color. While this particular tree had continued to grow taller and taller, it had never produced a single blossom. She said that George was so dismayed by the tree's inability to blossom that he planned to cut it down in the spring and plant a new one. He loved color and wanted to see blossoms from their breakfast table.

We were still feeling hopeful as we drove to the hospital, but encountered a radically different situation upon our arrival. George had taken a turn for the worse and his organs were failing. God was calling to him, and we knew that his remaining time on earth was short. My mom, Larry, and I decided to let him pass into the next world with dignity and love. We removed the feeding tube and chose not to place him on a ventilator. We each expressed our deep love for George and each gave him permission to leave. We held each other and held George as his spirit peacefully left this world.

The following morning, as we sat down for coffee at my mom's breakfast table, we looked out the window and gasped. Their once forlorn Bradford pear tree was bursting with color. This tree, which had been barren just twenty-four hours earlier, was now filled beyond capacity with large, beautiful, perfect pink blossoms.

These colorful blossoms stayed on that tree until well after frost had felled the blossoms of neighboring trees. When this tree finally began to drop its leaves, it did so on the side facing away from the window before dropping a single blossom on the side that faced my mother's breakfast window. What a gift from my stepfather. What a miracle. My mother subsequently commissioned a painting of that tree, with its bounty of blossoms, which she gave to me in celebration of George and of our shared experience. I have hung this painting in my bathroom dressing area and it gives me a deep sense of peace and contentment every time I look at it.

My return trip to Jackson Hole was taxing, but calm. No fire alarms or other such unexpected difficulties. When I finally arrived in my driveway, I saw the great grey owl land once again. It settled onto a post within arm's reach of me and we fondly regarded each other. With tears in my eyes and gratitude in my heart, I recognized the angel within the owl and gave thanks for the compassionate guidance it had given me.

I have never seen that owl since. Its presence reminded me once again that God loves us, directs our steps, and is always available to us in one manner or another. Truly, God's messengers are everywhere and come to us in the forms that we can and will accept. That may mean a great grey owl or other sort of creature to one person, and a human being to another.

As I mentioned earlier in this book when describing one of my conversations with an angel in a sundrenched field in heaven, there are angels all around us and we each have "personal" angels who watch over us all day, every day. They help us, nudge us, and guide us in all sorts of little ways that we usually don't notice. Sometimes they push us forward and sometimes they pull us backward. Always, they want very much for us to follow the path that has been laid out for us by God.

CHAPTER 22

INSPIRATION TO OTHERS

"I will praise you, Lord, with all my heart.
I will tell of all the marvelous
things you have done.
I will be filled with joy because of you.
I will sing praises to your name,
O Most High."

—Psalm 9:1–2 (NLT)

୭

A couple of months later, when I had physically recovered some and become a little more mobile, I was asked to speak to groups at several local churches. There was great interest in hearing my story, and I was happy to share my experience of God's miraculous interventions in my life. Portions of my story have been recounted on many occasions since then, and by numerous people. An audio recorded version of my original presentation is still being circulated. I see this continued interest in my story as a demonstration of people's desire to be inspired by, and believe in, the possibility of God's intervention.

It is often difficult to believe that an all-powerful God could possibly care about each one of us individually or be willing to directly intervene in our lives. I am a scientist. I understand numbers and statistics. I am skeptical and a bit cynical. There are so many of God's creations on this planet and we are each so small. I wonder how any individual can be significant when compared to the universe and how it could be possible for God to know us individually, let alone love us deeply and intercede when necessary.

What a scientist cannot account for is the alteration of time and space and dimension that is God's. I certainly cannot understand how it works, but I have experienced it and I accept that each one of us is a special and valued child of God. We are humans and do not have the capacity to understand God or begin to understand God's capabilities. Consider this as a paltry example: Does a parent with multiple children run out of love? Does that same parent value one child less just because they also have other children, or do they love the child less who occasionally makes them angry? The answer to all of these hypothetical questions, of course, is "no." The more we love, the more love we have to offer. So it is with God's love for us. It is inexhaustible.

God definitely knows each one of us. I mean "know" in an absolute, complete, and pure sense: like a seamstress knows her dress when she has grown the cotton from a seed, spun the cotton fibers into thread, woven the fabric, and stitched the fabric together to make a dress; or like a carpenter knows the chair that he has crafted by hand from a tree that he himself planted, nurtured, and felled. God knew each one of us even before He sent us into our mother's womb.

Not only did the telling of my story give others inspiration and hope, it also freed a great many people to tell their own stories. I cannot count the number of people who have approached me or called me, asking for a couple of minutes of my time. Each one of them begins their conversation the same way: "I want to tell you about something that happened to me . . . I never told anyone about it because I didn't think anyone would believe me." Then each proceeds to tell me of an extraordinary experience that occurred in which they interacted with angels, communicated with God's messengers, or spent time with spirits. Each of them feels liberated after telling me of their experiences, and it is clear that each feels validated by talking to me.

The human brain is quite good at remembering events, but not usually so adept at remembering the precise details. If you ask most people to describe their wedding, a child's birth, or other such important life events, the tiny details will have faded and the stories will likely have changed some over time. Think about fisherman's tales, which grow with each telling, or the old-time game of "telephone" in which a story is whispered from one person to the next. The last person in line tells the story out loud and, when compared to the original version, is usually full of notable differences. Even vivid dreams rarely stay in our memories for more than a few minutes.

I have observed one of the truly remarkable and consistent aspects of accounts of experiences that involve the presence or intervention of God is that the description of the experience remains constant no matter how much time has elapsed. People who have been involved in a godly experience remember with clarity and constancy the details of the incident and vividly recall their emotions as though they had just occurred.

The stories of almost everyone who has spoken with me began with some sort of traumatic situation. This is fairly predictable, and it is unfortunate that we rarely have such intense spiritual connections except under conditions of dire stress. I believe that anyone can have the same connections and experiences that I have had, but I think we are too distracted by the world around us when we are under "normal" circumstances. When we are in dire circumstances, these distractions quickly fall away and we are able to discern that which is most important: our relationship with God.

Under ordinary circumstances, it is usually quite difficult to voluntarily remove these distractions in order to experience God. Paul Hayden, my minister, likens it to the frequencies on a radio. We must tune our soul to the "right frequency" in order to hear the messages being sent to us from God.

One day after I had recovered enough to return to my medical practice, a woman I knew arrived at my office without an appointment. She knew it was my busiest day of the work week, but she insisted on speaking with me. Now, to understand this part of the story, you must understand our shared history. Shortly after I began my medical practice in Wyoming, this woman's husband came to me for care. He underwent a major surgery, which I performed, and had no difficulties. His hospital course after surgery was entirely uncomplicated; he felt great and by the third day, I was beginning to plan his discharge from the hospital.

Unbeknownst to me, my patient and his wife had visited with their Latter-Day Saints bishop prior to this surgery and had received blessings from him. He had told my patient's wife that she would have to give up the thing that she loved the most. He told my patient that God was very pleased with him, that the veil between this world and the next would be very thin, and that he would be required to make a choice.

Before surgery, my patient and his wife had discussed together their interpretation of these blessings. They had concluded that my patient would have to choose between continued life on earth or physical death. They were both spiritually devoted and knew that my patient would choose God. On the fourth day after his surgery, my patient suddenly dropped dead while in the bathroom. His wife later told me that throughout the day of his passing, her husband had been speaking with angels who he said were in the room with them. He kept asking her if she could see them and was disappointed that she couldn't. He told her how much he loved and valued her as a wife, but that he had to go with the angels and that he would visit her.

Now back to the story. Given this background, and the fact that she had driven several hours to see me, I could not refuse her request for a bit of my time. We sat in the outdoor courtyard and she apologized profusely for interrupting my day, but she had something of great importance to tell me. She was very worried that something terrible was about to happen to me, and she felt like she needed to warn me. She told me that in the time since her husband's death, his spirit would occasionally visit their home and give her guidance. She had not seen him for many months, but he had come into her dreams the day before she drove to my office.

During this visitation, her husband had been excited and jubilant. He told her that I had been in a terrible accident and that he had asked the Heavenly Father if he could be one of those sent to save me. As he described it to her, his request had been honored and he was so pleased to have been able to walk beside me and lift me up during that time.

His wife had not known anything of my boating accident in Chile, but she was able to give details of the scene that were known only to those who were present. After she completed her story and added her plea that I be careful, I told her the story of my accident. Although she was startled by the past tense of my story, she was not shocked by the story itself, as her husband had already told her many of the same details.

CHAPTER 23

GOD ROLLS THE STONE AWAY

**"Praying in faith is not an inner conviction
that God will act according to our desires
if only we believe hard enough. It involves
believing that God will always respond to
our prayers in accord with His nature,
His purposes, and His promises."**

—Alvin VanderGriend

୬

After my kayaking accident, I felt as though I
didn't belong in the world and felt isolated. I was
depressed at being on earth and was consumed
with trying to understand what had happened
to me and what I was supposed to do with the
knowledge I gained. In trying to understand my
experience, I read many accounts of other people's near-death experiences. I found some comfort in knowing that my emotions, reactions and
frustrations were common after this sort of ex-

perience. I, like so many others who have experienced death, no longer felt the pull of earthly concerns.

As a result, I became limitlessly more tolerant of the behavior of others but far less tolerant of my personal involvement with them. I had always sought total integration in my life, but now I was driven to such. It was my goal always to be an honest, ethical, and godly woman in my personal life, my family life, and my professional life. I intended to live a prayerful life of thanksgiving and joy and it became increasingly important to me that I spend my time with like-minded people.

Bill and I both became increasingly frustrated by the attitudes and behavior of some of our medical partners and by 2004, we thought it best if we charted our own course. We wanted out, but leaving our medical group was a risky decision for us. It was the only orthopaedic group in town and everyone in the partnership had signed a "non-compete" agreement. We felt justified in leaving, but it was possible that our non-compete agreement would be enforced and we would need to leave town in search of work.

We were struggling with our uncertainty when we left in the spring for a family vacation to Virgin Gorda, an island in the British Virgin Islands.

We were still anxious about it when we awoke on Easter morning, but God tells us not to fear, and promises, "I am with you, I will strengthen you, I will help you, I will uphold you." In keeping with God's promises, Easter morning proved to be a new beginning for our family. We went to a sermon in the resort's beachside conference room, where we listened to an energetic island preacher whose charisma enveloped the gathering. He did not preach on the usual topics of Jesus' death and resurrection. He chose to speak about the fear felt by the guards and about the power of God on that day of Christ's resurrection. He pointed out that the Romans were so afraid of Jesus, despite their claims of His being nothing special, that they securely sealed his tomb and posted guards on all sides.

On the third day after Jesus' death, there was a violent earthquake as an angel of the Lord came down from heaven and rolled back the stone to Jesus' tomb. The point the preacher made when discussing this story was that when God is involved, nothing can prevent the stone from being rolled away. Bill and I felt that God was involved in our lives and that it was time to roll away our stone and be set free. As soon as we left the service, we electronically submitted our letters of resignation to our office manager. We were ecstatic when we received confirmation of their receipt and celebrated the coming of our unknown future.

Within a couple of months, we moved into our own offices and formed a new medical practice together. We have never looked back. When God is present, things happen. Our practice thrived and when Dr. Alvis Forbes returned from his military service in the Gulf War, he also left our previous orthopaedic group and joined us. A man of great integrity, he shared our commitment to an integrated, God-centered way of life and we knew we had made the right choice.

CHAPTER 24

WILLIE

**"God's plan and His ways of working out
His plans are frequently beyond our ability
to fathom and understand. We must learn
to trust when we don't understand."**

—Jerry Bridges

∾

Much of what I was told by the angel in the field
had to do with my oldest son, Willie. Before I
introduce you to Willie, I need to categorically
state, once again, that I believe very young children clearly remember where they came from
and are still quite connected to God's world. I
believe they easily recall the images, knowledge,
and the love of the world they inhabited before
their birth. I believe children may still be able to
see angels, and many other people have written
about this phenomenon. As young children become more engaged with the world, their memo-

ries fade and they begin their personal journey, often filled with detours and dead-ends, of finding their way back to God. Ultimately, they must not only find God, but must freely choose to accept God's love and direction. God gave humans this ability to choose freely, which makes us ultimately responsible for our choices, our actions, and our lives.

Free choice requires that a person first understand that the choice he or she makes is fully theirs and that they are not being "made" to choose by something or someone other than themselves. It also requires that they choose between two or more alternatives, only one of which can be realized at a given time. For example, a person can choose to accept or reject a dinner invitation but cannot do both at the same time. As described by scholars of psychology, this inability to simultaneously choose more than one alternative creates internal emotional conflict. This internal conflict has been shown to lead to a person's greater examination of their choices, with resulting increased perceived value and a stronger embrace of his or her final choice.

Each person can choose God or reject God but cannot choose to do both simultaneously. By freely choosing to believe God's promises, a person's faith may be more strongly embraced and, therefore, less likely to falter in times of struggle, sadness, or other such difficulties.

During my initial hospitalization after my accident in Chile, when I was speaking with Jesus in the sun-drenched field, I asked him why everyone on earth wasn't given the opportunity to have the same experience that I was having. It seemed that if everyone shared this experience, hatred would disappear, we would be better stewards of the earth, eradicate hunger, no longer wage wars, and generally treat one another better on a daily basis. I no longer remember the angel's exact words, but his amused response reiterated Jesus' comments to Thomas: "Because you have seen me, you have believed; blessed are those who have not seen and yet have believed" **(John 20:29, NIV).**

That is not to say that older children and adults have no memory. It seems that God sends us to earth with a deeply-rooted desire to seek meaning and spirituality, and until we satisfy this desire, we experience a void in our souls. Some people fill this void with God, some fill it with material possessions or other worldly desires, and some try not to feel this void by deadening their senses with drugs or alcohol.

It is with this understanding of my belief that I will tell this next part of my story. Willie and I had always been very close and I always felt a sense of deep spiritual connection with his soul. When he was young, perhaps four or five, he and I were chatting before bed. I do not recall what prompted the comment, but I said something about, "When you are eighteen . . ."

Willie looked startled and said, "But I'm not going to be eighteen."

I asked him "What did you say?" with a somewhat joking tone. He looked back at me with serious intensity, curiosity, and disbelief, as he said, "You know. I'm never going to be eighteen. That's the plan. You know that." He said it as though I must be kidding with him. Surely, I must know the plan for his life.

This exchange was like a knife to my heart. I never forgot it and did not dismiss it. I cherished each subsequent day I had with this son, wondering which one would be his last.

In the years following my boating accident, I intermittently thought about my conversation with Jesus regarding Willie and contemplated the reasons for my return to earth. Given Willie's long-ago stated certainty that he would not reach the age of eighteen, I assumed that the expectations regarding Willie had less to do with his protection and more to do with my expected role in helping my husband and my family after Willie's death. Not wanting to burden others with these thoughts, I held them inside and did not tell anyone. It seemed to become a waiting game, but as the date of Willie's eighteen birthday neared, I became filled with anticipatory grief.

I finally told my husband about my conversation with our son that had occurred so many years earlier. I'm not sure that he was glad to share my burden of worry, but it certainly made me feel just a little bit better to tell him about it.

On a Saturday night during the summer before Willie's eighteenth birthday, I had a dream in which a boy, who I did not know, told me that he had "traded places with Willie." I awoke confused and bewildered. I was quite startled later in the day to discover that the boy in my dream, a well-liked and well-respected young man in our community, had been killed the prior afternoon in a motor vehicle accident while on his way to a swim meet. I felt guilty and conflicted in my emotions. I was filled with sadness at another family's loss, but relieved that perhaps our family would be spared.

A couple of months later, we received a phone call telling us of the tragic news that one of our dear friends died suddenly and unexpectedly while in a hunting camp. Four days later, we received a similar call telling us of the sudden and unexpected death of Alvis, our medical partner. They were both dear friends and bigger-than-life sorts of people who had been active in the Jackson Hole community for many years. We were devastated, the community was reeling, and our office was a place of mourning.

In our country, we no longer seem to have funerals; instead we have "celebrations of life." But truly, the only person who ever celebrates is the one who died. Those who have died experience the joy of returning to the glory of God's world, while the people left behind are sad, lonely, and rarely feel joyful about the occasion.

I am not superstitious, but events frequently occur in threes. Our community was mourning three deaths. Could this be another indication that Willie's long ago prediction would come to nothing? This question was on my heart one month prior to his birthday, when Willie, Eliot, and Betsy left home to attend a ski camp in Sweden. The three of them drove to Salt Lake City where they spent the night before going to the airport early the following morning.

After they checked their bags, Eliot and Betsy stayed at the airport while Willie drove back to the hotel, where he had originally planned to leave the car parked. When he realized that he did not have enough time to return to the hotel and take the shuttle back to catch the flight, he decided to return to the parking lot at the airport and leave the car there. On his way back to the airport, he exited the freeway and stopped behind a few cars that were lined up at a red light on the exit ramp. His foot slipped off the brake, and the car moved forward several feet, gently striking the bumper of the car in front of him. He didn't think this was a serious problem, but got out of his car anyway and walked up to the other car. The other driver had not moved his car to the side of the roadway, did not get out of his car, did not open his window, and would not look at Willie.

Confused by this driver's behavior, Willie returned to his own car, pulled to the side of the road, and called me on his cell phone. Thinking that maybe the other driver had not seen Willie or even noticed that his car had been struck—although why else would he have stopped on the exit ramp? I suggested that Willie return to the other car and tap on the window to get the other driver's attention. He did so, but got the same result.

He returned to his car and, again, called me. I suggested that Willie write our insurance information on a piece of paper to give to the other driver, walk to the car while keeping me on the phone, and offer to have me speak with the other driver. I listened from my end of the phone line as Willie walked to the car for the third time and asked the driver if he would speak with me. I heard silence followed by a piercing scream.

The other driver had produced a handgun and was pointing it directly at Willie. Willie was frozen with fear, but fortunately his phone was frozen to his ear. As a result, I did not have to overcome his screaming to speak to him. I was able to speak directly into his brain: "Run, get in your car, turn the key in the ignition, drive away, do **not** stop!"

I certainly do not know if my son would have been shot had I not been on the phone with him when the other driver pointed his gun at Willie. What I do know, however, is that I am the only person who could have broken through to Willie's brain and given him instructions that he would unquestioningly follow. I believe that on that day in Salt Lake City, my son reached a branch point in his life that led either to the death he had predicted so many years earlier or to his continued life. Despite the angel's earlier words that I would need to be a rock of support for my family and community after Willie's death, I felt like the plan for Willie had changed. Because I was alive, Willie stayed alive.

CHAPTER 25

BILL

**"We know that all things
Work together for good
To those who love God."**

—Romans 8:28 (NKJV)

∾

I was also sent back to earth to protect the health of my husband. Recall that two of our dear friends had recently died unexpectedly, and both of presumed heart attacks. They were both men about the same age as my husband: fifty-three years old. Like my husband, both men were physically fit and active and neither man smoked cigarettes, drank alcohol, or used recreational drugs. Neither "should" have died. Both had close and loving families as well as deep faith.

I did not want Bill to walk down the same road as these men, so I started pestering him to have an evaluation of his heart. Had I not returned to

earth after my boating accident and been present to prod him, Bill doubts he would even have
considered being evaluated. But I was there, so he
was evaluated. He had a calcium-scoring CT scan
in December 2007; a specialized test that specifically evaluates the amount of calcium present in
the blood vessels of the heart. It is a non-invasive
way of determining if coronary artery disease is
present and, if so, to what degree.

The good news was that his heart looked
perfect: no calcium, no coronary artery disease.
When they performed the scan, however, the
doctors had slightly misaligned the scanner. It
was off-center by just a fraction and on the very,
very edge of the resulting images the radiologist
saw a small nodule in Bill's lung tissue.

Hoping that it was evidence of an infection,
Bill was placed on antibiotics. At home we racked
our brains trying to think of any unusual expo-
sure he may have had to asbestos, tuberculosis,
or one of the other types of lung infections that
were frequently seen in his birthplace of Southern California. A few days later, when a repeat
CT scan of his lungs showed no change in the
images, he underwent a CT-guided biopsy. The
results showed a malignant tumor of the lung.
We arranged for removal of this tumor, which
was able to be done thoracoscopically. He was

discharged from the hospital after only one day and he was gently skiing within a week. He has gone on to recover fully and his follow-up CT scans have confirmed the absence of any recurrence. His positive outcome is likely due to the very small size of the tumor at the time of its discovery.

Throughout our lives, we are conditioned to see each of the events of this sequence in isolation, and to think of them as "coincidental" or "lucky." When you consider the entire sequence of events, however, it is difficult to discount the possibility of it being miraculous. Had our two good friends not died, I would not have insisted on an evaluation. Had I died on the Chilean river, Bill would likely not have had a heart evaluation. Based on the tumor type, had the scan not been misaligned, the mass would not have been found until it was larger, making it too late to hope for a cure. If the identified mass had been two millimeters smaller, it would not have been visible on the scan. Three millimeters larger, and it would have put Bill into a far more ominous statistical category, with a much worse prognosis. Without my return from heaven after my boating accident, our four children might have become orphans. At the time, I believed this was the protection of my family for which I had been sent back.

CHAPTER 26

CHAD

**"For by grace you have been
saved through faith,
And this is not your own doing;
It is the gift of God."**

—Ephesians 2:8 (NRS)

∾

Chad Long was a delightful young man, but I did not know him well prior to my trip to Chile. His spiritual faith had been another explanation given to me for my return to earth, and I was told I would play an important role in his becoming a godly man. For years this was a source of great confusion for me, for I already believed Chad to be a godly man; He had been born into a Christian family, had married a Christian woman, and was never shy about discussing the role God played in his and his family's life. Although I knew what I had been told by the angel, I really couldn't imagine what I could contribute to Chad's faith.

In preparing for the writing of this book, I spoke individually with each of the Longs. I asked them to recount, without my interruptions or comments, their recollections of the circumstances of my boating accident and to also recall their emotions. Chad gave me his account and, as he was describing the effect the events had on his life, he disclosed that for the several years leading up to my trip to Chile he had been "in a bad place." He had not been the person he wanted to be, and felt that he had been suffering the age-old battle between God and Satan. Before going to Chile in the winter of 1999, he had been struggling in an unhealthy relationship and was lying to himself and others about the type of person he was becoming.

At the end of the Chilean boating season the year Bill and I went, Chad returned to Idaho with memories of my accident, but also re-entered the same unhealthy relationship and personal environment he had left. He wrestled with his faith, especially with the question of how to be a godly man. He said that when he allowed himself to contemplate the experiences and miracles related to my accident, he began to understand and believe that if a person can let go of the earthly logistics of life, live in faith, and give control to God, great things can happen and the supernatural can occur. Without God, our options are limited.

He points to my boating accident as a major turning point in his life; the point at which he became comfortable in his faith and comfortable in his relationship with God. It resulted in his consciously choosing to make the changes necessary to live a godly life.

Chad is now reconciled with God, is no longer afraid to alienate people by being open about his faith, and he relies on God to direct his life. Speaking with him about the impact of my accident on his life resolved my long-standing confusion about what the angel had told me, and I am profoundly grateful to have been an instrument through which God called to him.

CHAPTER 27

COMPULSION TO WRITE

"Whether you turn to the right or to the left,
Your ears will hear a voice
behind you, saying,
'This is the way; Walk in it.'"

—Isaiah 30:21 (NIV)

༄

Life in our household is hectic and usually bustling with activity. We each have a variety of interests and endeavors, which makes our daily home life exciting, interesting, and satisfying, if not always predictable. By early 2009, I had lived up to what I believe were many of God's expectations for my life and I felt content. My husband was healthy, our three younger kids were active, happy, and blossoming into wonderful young people, and Willie, our oldest child, was positively flourishing.

In the period after his eighteenth birthday, Willie led a joyful, albeit frenzied life. He had a terrific season of Nordic skiing, winning his seventh and eighth Wyoming State Championships (a record for which he was featured in **Sports Illustrated** "Faces in the Crowd"). He also expanded the non-profit environmental organization he created to promote local "no-idling" policies and enlisted the support of many local businesses for this cause. He strongly believed that encouraging people to make a conscious, environmentally-based choice about turning off their car engines would prompt them to think about their other choices as well; even small choices can make a difference when added together. He believed that we are each the ripple of hope described in Robert Kennedy's 1966 speech at the University of Capetown, South Africa:

> **"It is from numberless diverse acts of courage and belief that human history is shaped. Each time a man stands up for an ideal, or acts to improve the lot of others, or strikes out against injustice, he sends forth a tiny ripple of hope, and crossing each other from a million different centers of energy and daring those ripples build a current which can sweep down the mightiest walls of oppression and resistance."**

Willie was intrigued by the political process as a means for change and in 2008, when he was only eighteen years old, he was elected by members of our community to be a Wyoming delegate to the Democratic National Convention in Denver, Colorado. Willie's sincerity, energy, and never-ending flow of ideas for living responsibly and making the world a better place for all was enormously contagious. He was passionate about making a difference in our world and inspired those around him to care about issues, to get involved, and to become better people in the process. It didn't matter to him what a person's "issue" was; he just wanted people to get involved and make a difference. I admired his passion and could not have been more delighted with the man Willie was becoming.

Despite my reasonable sense of contentment, I knew I had at least one big job left to do before I could truly rest contented in God's presence: I was supposed to share my life stories and experiences by talking about them and writing about them. I knew that I had been given the many experiences of my life, my death, and my return so that I could use my experiences and observations to help others stop doubting and just believe—believe that spiritual life is more important than our physical one. Believe that God is present and at work in our lives and our world. Believe that we are each a beautiful part of an intricate tapestry of creation. Believe there is no such thing as "coincidence."

I knew what I was supposed to do; I just didn't want to do it.

In the years after my boating accident, I easily followed God's edict of being joyful always, praying without ceasing, and giving thanks in all circumstances. My experiences with God were a part of every breath I took (I even named my new bicycle "Breath of Life"). I never stopped feeling gratitude for the blessings I had received; I just didn't feel like writing about them. I did feel increasing guilt about not completing my task and for even thinking about it as a "task" rather than a privilege. I felt increasing guilt for not living up to what I imagined were God's expectations for me. I felt mounting pressure to write my story, but I just kept putting it on the bottom of the nagging list of things that I needed/wanted to get done . . . organizing the garage, clearing the closets of no longer used clothing, getting Christmas cards out on time, being better about writing/calling my family, organizing photo albums, and so on.

I am quite good at procrastinating, so I kept living my life as usual until, quite unexpectedly in the spring of 2009, I was awakened in the early hours by an overpowering need to put my story into words. It consumed me entirely. I popped out of bed at four or five each morning (the only hours during which I could write without being interrupted) and marveled at how effortlessly the words poured out of me and onto the computer screen. I would feverishly write for a couple of hours before starting our family's morning routine of getting ready for school and work. In one week, the first draft of this book was finished. I was emotionally drained, but quickly worked through a couple of revisions before losing motivation once again.

It was a busy time for my family and I let this manuscript languish for a couple of months while I focused on the activities of our daily lives. Peter was finishing his second year in middle school. Betsy was finishing her junior year of high school and Eliot was contemplating his college choices while preparing for his high school graduation. Willie was temporarily living in Washington, D.C., enjoying all the city has to offer, and Bill and I continued to work while trying to keep everyone's schedules organized.

Willie completed his time in Washington then returned to Wyoming to help celebrate Eliot's graduation on May 29, 2009.

The brothers planned to leave Jackson Hole the following weekend to begin their next adventure; they planned to drive across the country and live together in Northern Maine while ski training for six months with the Maine Winter Sports Club. The day before their departure, Willie asked me about writing a will. He wanted to know who writes a will, why a person would write a will, and whether he should write one. He also wanted to know if I had a life insurance policy for him and, upon discovering that I had never thought of it, wanted to know how I could get one. He really pestered me about it. Although I felt strange having this conversation with a healthy nineteen-year-old, I assured him that I would look into the matter.

Emotionally, I am even-keeled and I have never been particularly emotional when any of my kids began something new or left for an adventure. I have always been excited for them and have known that we would stay in communication. The morning my two boys left for Maine was different. Willie's Subaru was overloaded with most of their worldly possessions and as I watched them making their final preparations I felt tears welling up in my eyes. I'm not sure why, but it reminded me of the day I took Willie to his first preschool class. On that day, which now seems like a different lifetime, he gave me a kiss, then confidently left my side and walked through the classroom door. As I watched him walk up the sidewalk and into his future, the symbolism of it all overwhelmed me and I shocked myself by crying most of the way home.

As the boys and I stood next to the Subaru saying "good-bye," I kept telling them how much I loved them, told them to be careful driving, to call me from the road, and other such things mothers generally say in those moments. When we embraced, I started crying and almost couldn't let them go. I remember holding Willie just a little bit longer than I normally would have, looking directly into his eyes and telling him how much I loved him and what an extraordinary young man he had become. I told them both how proud Bill and I were of them and what a great adventure they would have together. They drove off and, despite speaking with them many times each day while they were on the road, I still felt entirely out of sorts.

Perhaps I was uneasily awaiting a future that I had already seen.

CHAPTER 28

THE LONGEST DAY
OF THE YEAR

**"And be sure of this:
I am with you always,
Even to the end of the age."**

—Matthew 28:20 (NLT)

∽

The boys arrived in Fort Kent, Maine, and settled into a routine. They lived in the training center with several other athletes and were excited about the training program. They trained hard and shared a lot of laughs as they explored their new surroundings. Friends of ours, Sophie and Derek, whose children had attended school with the boys, own a fishing lodge not far from where the boys were living. The lodge is in Canada, on the banks of the Grand Cascapedia River. The pace of life there is relaxed and filled with activities like swimming, fishing from canoes, playing games, and making maple syrup hearts while telling stories around a campfire. Sophie and Derek's family spends time there each summer and the boys happily accepted their gracious invitation to visit.

On one afternoon, Willie was fishing in a canoe with Sophie and two of her beautiful golden retrievers, Rusty and Lucky. Sophie is an exceptionally loving and supportive person who enjoyed listening to, and encouraging, all of Willie's many, many ideas for the future. Knowing that his life was more than full and usually moved at an extremely rapid pace, Sophie was surprised to see that Willie was a calm and graceful fisherman. He wasn't bored and didn't seem to care whether or not he actually caught a fish; he was simply enjoying the surrounding beauty and the ebb and flow of the river while chatting with her. Seemingly out of the blue, Willie asked Sophie what she knew about the soul. She went on to tell him that she believes the soul is the essence of being that has a direct connection to God. She told him that she believes our souls are timeless and come to earth in order to learn something new or otherwise attain spiritual growth.

Willie seemed quite interested in her thoughts, asked several more questions, then quietly seemed to contemplate what she had said. He then told her how happy he was and how grateful he was for the wonderful life he had lived. They soon paddled to where Sophie's son was standing on the river bank and when they got out of the canoe, she marveled at Willie's ability to seamlessly transition from their deep discussion of the soul to playfully hanging out with his buddy. Willie awoke the next day and ate his usual five pieces of bacon, four eggs, two pieces of toast, and pancakes with homemade maple syrup before returning to Fort Kent with Eliot to resume their ski training.

In the early hours of June 21, 2009, I again felt an absolute compulsion to finish this manuscript and an intense pressure to complete my work. By early in the afternoon, I finally completed what I believed would be the final version of my manuscript. The intensity of the elation I felt when I clicked the "save" button and shut down my computer was something I had never before felt and have trouble adequately describing. There was an explosion of freedom within my soul. I felt light and happy and magnificent. I was filled with relief at having competed this task and grateful for the experiences leading up to it. I had been obedient to God. Life could not have seemed better.

I was still feeling lighthearted as my youngest son, Peter, and I were driving into town later that day. We decided to tease Eliot about something, so called him from my car. I must have accidentally hit the speaker button on my phone, for when the call was answered by an unfamiliar voice Peter was also able to hear that person's words. We asked for Eliot, but the man on the other end of the call told us his name and said that Eliot could not speak. Although there had been no amusement in his voice, we thought he was trying to be funny. I hadn't actually recognized the caller's name, so I thought it was one of the other skiers in the training program. I asked him to stop kidding around and give the phone to Eliot. He again said his name (it was one of the boys' ski coaches), and told me that Willie had been involved in a roller skiing accident and was dead.

As I tried to control the rising panic that was beginning to cloud my brain and constrict my breathing, I told him to stop joking around, that it was not funny, and again asked him to please hand the phone to Eliot. This conversation repeated itself again and again as I immediately turned the car around and raced home. I really couldn't even comprehend the words that he was saying. I ran into our house and screamed for my husband to "talk to this man because I don't even know what he is saying!"

Our world was forever changed.

CHAPTER 29

MY BEAUTIFUL SON

**"Be still,
And know that I am God."**

—Psalm 46:10 (NKJV)

❧

On the other side of the country, the same day had begun with a similar sense of joy. Willie spent the morning with Eliot, and then met their friend Hilary (another skier) in the afternoon at her family's home in Fort Fairfield. They planned to spend the afternoon restoring a rusty old bicycle they picked up at a garage sale earlier in the summer, then roller ski for a couple of hours before having dinner with her family. If you are unfamiliar with them, roller skis are a dry-land version of cross country ski equipment. They look a little bit like very short skis, with ski bindings mounted on the top and polyethylene wheels at either end. An athlete can then use them to "ski" on pavement, with or without the use of ski poles. They are used by Nordic skiers to increase endurance, work on technique, and develop ski-specific strength when there is no snow.

June 21, 2009, was the summer solstice, the longest day of the year, and it was a beautiful time in New England. As they skied past a cemetery, Willie told Hilary the story of how he had told me when he was very young that he would not reach his eighteenth birthday and of my coming to his West Yellowstone hotel room at 4 A.M. the morning of his birthday just to hug him and verify that he was alive. They went on to talk about death and what it meant to each of them. He then became quite specific in describing his feelings about death and told Hilary what he wanted done in the event of his death. He was clear, for example, about his desire to be cremated. He expressed his opinion that using land for burial was not consistent with his love for the planet and his passion about being a responsible steward of the land.

As they skied toward their half-way point, they crested a hill overlooking a beautiful river. The sun was setting and the golden rays of light played on the water, the trees, and the distant hills, creating a magical quality to the scene as they stopped to take it all in. Willie's final comment as they resumed skiing was, "If we died, wouldn't this be an incredible last vision?" Less than three minutes later, Willie was dead.

Erik, a Fort Fairfield youth who had celebrated his eighteenth birthday just weeks earlier, had decided to "just drive around" that evening. When his car approached the section of road upon which Hilary and Willie were skiing, they both heard the car engine and moved as far to the right side of the road as was possible. They continued skiing along the road's edge and waited for the car to drive by. This is something every Nordic skier has experienced thousands of times during their off-season training. As they waited for the car to pass, they could not have known that Erik was distracted by his cell phone. For the almost-quarter-mile of clear vision of Hilary and Willie he would have had if he were paying attention while he was driving, he saw nothing.

Erik missed hitting Hilary, who was skiing behind Willie, by only a few inches. Startled, she looked up and watched in horror as Erik's speeding car stuck Willie from behind. My beautiful son was killed instantly.

CHAPTER 30

THE OTHER SIDE
OF TIME

"Remind me each morning of
your constant love,
For I put my trust in you.
My prayers go up to you;
Show me the way I should go."

—Psalm 143:8 (GNT)

෴

By midnight on the twenty-first of June, thanks
to God's grace and the efforts and graciousness
of a local acquaintance and philanthropist, Bill,
Peter, myself, our family's minister, and our dear
friends Dave and Ellen, who "just happened"
to be at a point in their careers where they were
able to suddenly drop everything and leave town,
were being propelled through the blackness of
the night sky on a private flight to Maine. Our
daughter, Betsy, who had been visiting friends in
Vermont, was being driven by them to Fort Fair-

field, and Eliot was staying with Hilary's family. After a night of disbelief, they, along with Eliot, met us at the airport when we arrived early the next morning.

Willie died instantly, so he was never taken to a hospital. We drove directly to the funeral home and spent the long hours of the morning cleaning the blood from Willie's broken body, and anointing him with our tears and with our love. Through this time of unimaginable sorrow, God gently held us, loved us, and carried us.

We visited the site of Willie's death and I was struck by many emotions as we slowly examined and absorbed the details of the area. My first observation was that Willie was not there. I felt no deep connection or emotional reaction to the physical place. It merely felt like the place where his spirit had left this world. Secondly, I had the sense that he had tried to make it as nice a spot for us as was possible—accessible, identifiable, and beautiful. His crumpled body had landed in an area blanketed by blossoming wild alpine roses, overlooking a valley with a meandering stream and rolling green hills.

I'm not sure why it matters to me, but the site of Willie's death was as notable a site as one could wish for. God took our son, but there was no "grim reaper." I believe He sent his most gentle and loving angels to collect Willie's soul and take him to heaven.

Our days in Fort Fairfield moved quite slowly, with a decidedly altered sense of reality. Our faith, our minister, and our friends gave us the support and firm, but compassionate, guidance that allowed us to stagger through these days. Without them and the unqualified acceptance that our lives are all part of God's larger plan, it would have been nearly impossible to endure the trip to Maine or the very emotionally-draining journey home with Willie's ashes.

While in Maine, we had been protected and sheltered from people and telephones. As we traveled home, we became increasingly anxious about what the next days and weeks might bring. We had no desire to talk to anyone or see anyone. We really just wanted to stay in our isolated and insulated world of pain. It was, therefore, deeply emotional for us to be immediately pulled out of that world and into the thoughtful and compassionate support of our friends and neighbors the moment we arrived at our home; they had lined our front porch with a loving collection of flowering plants. Willie deeply appreciated the beauty of blossoming flowers, but he was never a big fan of cut flowers, as they serve such a transient role: cut, appreciated for a limited time, then being thrown out with the garbage. Our neighbors' decision to bring flowering plants in pots rather than cut flowers perfectly honored Willie and visually embraced us with their love.

Along with the flowers came the promise of planting them the next week in what would become a perennial flower garden. My only job was to decide where the flowers should be planted. Our home sits on six acres of previous ranchland. Other than wild grasses, the only vegetation consists of the trees, shrubs, and patches of domestic grass that we planted when we built and landscaped our house. It is not extensively landscaped, but I have always found great pleasure in walking around the property and studying the land. Willie and I often shared this pleasure together, and we enjoyed noting the many changes in color, shape, and fullness of the various plantings as the earth moved through its seasons.

In the days after our return from Maine, walking our property was the one activity that brought a small semblance of calm to my turbulent and broken spirit. As I walked, I tried to make sense of my life, contemplated what to say at my son's memorial service, and made detailed mental accountings of our property, trying to decide on a site for Willie's flowering garden. One morning, as I was walking past a small grouping of willow trees, I came upon a great surprise. The area around and within every willow was overflowing with the vivid, bold, deep pink-colored blossoms of wild Alpine roses. These flowers were of the exact color, shape, and appearance as had been the ones blooming in the field in which Willie died. Prior to visiting Willie's accident site, I had never seen one of these blossoms and I most definitely had never seen one on our property.

Willie knew the story of the pink blossoms on the Bradford pear tree that had appeared immediately after the death of my stepfather. He knew how significant and emotional that event had been for my mother and me, and he would have seen the painting of the tree hanging in my bathroom many, many times. I know that Willie sent us a message that day through the roses; one of appreciation, love, gratitude, and a sense of apology for leaving. I believe he knew this would be one of the few ways of communication we would not question.

Completing the story of the Bradford pear tree, after beautifully blooming for five years, it was suddenly and unexpectedly struck by lightning and destroyed, serving as a message telling my mother that it was "time to move forward" in her life. It makes me wonder if the beautiful Alpine roses that we now so lovingly nurture on our property will one day disappear.

CHAPTER 31

GIFTS OF COMPASSION

**"When I look into your eyes,
I know there is a God. Human
compassion and the capacity to love
are not the result of mere chance."**

—Charles W. Gerdts, III

∽

In the initial weeks following Willie's death, there were other gestures of love and gentleness that my family and I found comforting. One day, a notebook appeared on the bookshelf. In it were several letters that Willie had written on the eve of his nineteenth birthday, which was several months before his death.

He had written letters to some of his coaches and close friends, thanking them for the memories, their long-standing friendship and support, and for the impact they had on his life. His letters were from the heart and almost seemed like a "good-bye" letter; unusual for an eighteen year old. He also wrote letters, one to President-elect Obama and to Will-I-Am, a musician he admired; and one to President Lincoln in which he noted the sense of calm and deep inspiration that he felt when sitting in Lincoln's monument in Washington, D.C. Willie wrote that he felt like he could make a difference and that he could become the next Abraham Lincoln. He wanted to make "the **whole** world a better place."

Willie also wrote a letter to himself. In it, he talked about the great adventure his life had been. He observed that his life lacked simplicity, but guessed that was, "because there is so much to see and do in such a short time." He also wrote about how grateful he was for his family, his friends, his God, and for his faith. This letter was such a gift to me. It reassured me that Willie had a relationship with God, understood its importance, and was "right" with God before his death.

Willie had a way of making everyone feel special and feel that they each had a special relationship with him. After Willie's death, many people came forward to express their sadness and to express their gratitude for the life Willie led. They all mentioned ways he changed their lives for the better. Senator John Kerry called to express his condolences. He noted Willie's influence in his office, the changes that Willie inspired, and the impact he had on the Senator's staff. Senator Kerry also taped a video tribute for Willie's memorial service.

Singer-songwriter Carole King, who was also inspired by Willie's passion, sent us the following lyrics and music, which we played at his memorial service. Her song has given us a great deal of comfort, as the music is beautiful and the lyrics apt.

In the Name of Love

Do the things you believe in
In the name of love
And know that you aren't alone
We all have doubts and fears

Know throughout every season
You are the name of love
And you'll keep on feeling at home
Throughout the coming years

Change is for certain
This we all know
Each day opening the curtain
On a brand new show

Through your sorrow and grieving
Don't forget the name of love
It goes on without any end
Forever

Birth and life and death make a circle
We are all part of
To see the light everlasting
Live in the name of love
Forever

Community members wept and grieved with us. The skiing world was shocked and heartbroken. Hundreds of people from across the country came to Willie's memorial service, prayed with us and for us, and did what they could to lessen the pain. We met with our minister daily and were surrounded by close friends. I taped the following daily creed to our refrigerator and grasped onto it for survival.

My Daily Creed

I believe God's promises are true.
I believe heaven is real.
I believe nothing can separate me from God's love.
I believe God has work for me to do.
I believe God will see me through and carry me when I cannot walk.

God continued to carry our family month after month, as we struggled to put one foot in front of the other. I do not understand how anyone can make this journey without trusting in God's plan.

Growing up, I was taught that **Psalm 23:4** ("Though I walk through the valley of the shadow of death, I shall fear no evil. For you are with me; your rod and your staff, they comfort me") referred to one's own death and the dangerous journey back to God. Now I believe it actually refers to the people who are left behind to grieve. As grieving people walk through the valley of the shadow of a loved one's death, their sadness, confusion, anger, and despair can inadvertently prop open the door of their hearts, allowing evil to silently enter.

I had experienced death before—of grandparents, of parents, of friends—and I have found that grief is always a lonely, isolated process, as the death of a loved one carries different meaning to each person who is grieving. In those circumstances, however, it is usually possible to look to a spouse or other family member for support. The isolation of grief after the death of a child or a sibling is exponentially magnified by the fact that close family members who might otherwise be able to offer support are equally wrought with grief.

God's timing is always perfect and I think this may be why I was unmotivated to put my story into words before the spring of 2009. The writing of this manuscript was an emotionally intense experience for me. I had been very rigorous over the years with regard to restricting the amount of time I allowed myself to think about the events surrounding my own death and return to life. I love my life, I love my family dearly, and I know that my work on earth is not done. Despite that, recalling the alluring magnificence of God's world too vividly would make it easy to be consumed by a deep longing to return. I have always guarded my heart by not thinking about it too vividly or for too long. I imagine that this desire is similar to the deep longing recovering addicts must feel when they fondly recall the best times of their previous substance abuse. Anyway, I always found it emotionally draining and dangerous to spend too much time remembering not just the facts and events, but re-experiencing the actual emotions.

In writing this book, I allowed myself to fully embrace the spiritual experiences I had during my accident and its aftermath: reliving the details and immersing myself in the physical, emotional, and spiritual reality of that time. In doing so, I was freshly filled with the remembrance and acknowledgement of God's continuing and active presence in my life, His absolute grace, His pure love, and His promises for the future. I was, again, filled with the joy of His spirit and the knowledge that every event is a part of a larger and more beautiful tapestry.

Revisiting and re-experiencing these emotions and memories gave me the ability to be the physical, emotional, and spiritual rock of support that proved to be so essential for my family and my community after Willie's death. Perhaps if I had written this book several years earlier, I would not have so clearly remembered the words spoken to me by the angels or the many reasons for returning me to earth.

Bill and I were surprised to find that a predominant emotion during the first year was fear. Fear that we would never emerge from the emotional fog. Fear that we would never again be able to experience joy. Fear that we would fail our remaining children. Fear that we would forget. I think much of the fear and anxiety we felt was just fear of an unknown future that would not include the son that we loved so dearly. Someone told me, "When you love with all that you have, you grieve with all that you are," and I would certainly agree with this observation.

I did believe that God, if asked, would not only carry us, but also would protect our souls during this emotionally vulnerable time. Regardless, it was difficult for my husband to eradicate his feeling not just of sadness and fear, but of despair.

CHAPTER 32

PERFECT TIMING

"There is some good in the worst of us and some evil in the best of us. When we discover this, we are less prone to hate our enemies."

—Martin Luther King, Jr.

൭

I am an avid skier and eight months after Willie's death, my son Eliot and I were skiing in the back-country. This form of skiing involves placing synthetic animal skins on the bottom of one's skis, making it possible to climb up snowy mountainous terrain that is otherwise inaccessible. Upon reaching the summit, the skins are removed from the skis and the thrill of then skiing downhill, usually in fresh powdery snow, makes all of the uphill effort worthwhile. I love to amuse my kids, so at the end of the afternoon I was showing-off for Eliot, who was videotaping my skiing. I decided to ski over a gulley and try to "catch air"— not something I do well, but always something that makes Eliot and my other kids laugh. Rather than catching air, however, my skis twisted in different directions and I broke my ankle. At least Eliot was able to memorialize this with his video footage!

At this point my options were quite limited. I couldn't ski and Eliot couldn't carry me. We considered using our skis to make a sled but had to climb up a significant hill, so didn't think that was likely to be effective. I was already cold and I knew it would take at least several more hours for Eliot to ski out, contact the Search & Rescue team, and for them to return. I decided my only reasonable option was to tighten my ski boot (adding some stability to my ankle) and fortify myself for a slow, very painful hike/ski out of the back country. I used my ski poles and my good leg to carry me up and across the slopes, while hopelessly trying to let my injured one gently dangle. This journey back to our car took a couple of hours and was accompanied by a lifetime's worth of cursing. As an interesting side note, I had recently read a study by Stephens, Atkins, and Kingston in which they evaluated swearing as a response to pain (**NeuroReport,** August 5, 2009; volume 20, issue 12; 1056–60). In the study, two sets of data were collected based on how long volunteers were able to keep their arm submersed in ice water, a known pain stimulator, while either a commonplace word to describe a table or shouting the profanity of their choice. The authors found that volunteers had a significantly greater pain tolerance when using their profanity of choice. As I hiked the distance to our car, I performed my own personal experiment. I tried yelling words like "snow" and "tree" or yelling different profanities. In the end, I agreed whole-heartedly with the results of Stephens' study.

I had surgery that evening to repair my ankle and remained in the hospital overnight. A Rwandan priest named Father Ubald "just happened" to be visiting a friend in Jackson Hole at that time, and she brought him to the hospital to pray with me. To understand who Father Ubald is and what he represents, you must understand a little about his history.

The origins of the 1994 Rwandan genocide are complex and the ethnic divisions in Rwanda between the Hutus and Tutsis are longstanding. Tribal polarization exploded after the assassination of President Juvénal Habyarimana, who was a Hutu, and in a period of one hundred days, more than 800,000 people were systematically and violently murdered.

In the midst of this killing, Father Ubald, a Catholic priest whose Tutsi father had been murdered in the 1962 overthrow of the Rwandan government and who had been himself threatened by fellow seminarians in the 1980s, was forced to flee first to his bishop's residence and then to the Congo in return for a promise by the Hutus not to harm the people of his parish. As soon as he left, the Hutu members of his large parish betrayed this promise and brutally hacked to death approximately 45,000 Tutsi members of his parish. More than 80 members of his immediate and extended family, including his mother, were exterminated within the first two weeks of the massacre.

Before fleeing, Father Ubald promised his bishop that he would return to bring healing to his people. The massacre finally ended when the Rwandan Patriotic Front (RPF) regained power, but grief-stricken survivors were left bewildered by the intensity of the evil that had been unleashed in their country. Survivors of all ethnic groups experienced profound guilt: guilt for killing, guilt for surviving, guilt for not doing enough to prevent or mitigate the conflicts. Many sought revenge, but as has been said, "There is no revenge so complete as forgiveness."

Father Ubald spent many months in prayer and his tears filled a river before he made his way to Lourdes, France. It was there, as he meditated on the Stations of the Cross, that he heard God tell him to release his sorrows and "pick up his cross." God filled his heart with a forgiveness that can only come from God. Subsequently, he met with and forgave the mayor of his town, who was the man who ordered the murder of Father Ubald's own mother. Father Ubald took responsibility for that man's children, treating them as his own and even paying for their schooling.

Father Ubald is a man who radiates the purity of God's grace and preaches on forgiveness and reconciliation. He also holds healing masses, using his gifts to heal and renew others. He performs healing masses in Rwanda, Europe, and the United States. He is building a center in Rwanda, called The Secret of Peace, which will minister to the people of Rwanda and the surrounding areas of the Congo and Burundi, countries that have seen so much war, poverty, and trauma. He works tirelessly toward the goal of forgiveness, reconciliation, and peace for the people of Rwanda and throughout the world.

It was because of his background and experience in healing, that my friend, Katsey, brought him to my hospital room to pray over my ankle. When they arrived, I was so ill from the anesthetics and the pain medications that they quickly left. The following day, Father Ubald insisted that I visit him at Katsey's house once I was feeling better. I arranged a visit a few days later, and I brought Bill with me.

We chatted briefly, but then Father Ubald immediately focused on Bill. Together they prayed for more than an hour. I wanted to cry at the beauty of this, as I have never seen Bill be outwardly spiritual and this was an answer to many years of my prayers. The following week, Father Ubald had dinner in our home and the conversation turned to the topic of loss. Knowing his history of loss and grief makes listening to his thoughts quite compelling and powerful, so we were riveted as he described his own and his country's experiences with loss and the ongoing process of grief and forgiveness. He believes that the complex emotions related to loss almost always include some sort of anger or rage, guilt or shame that requires forgiveness before true healing, acceptance, and reconciliation can occur. Father Ubald also noted that forgiveness does not need to be two-sided. It comes from within a person and does not require the involvement, acknowledgment, or acceptance of the other.

As we discussed the many facets of forgiveness, I began to recognize that although I really did believe Willie's death was part of God's larger plan, I felt anger, and perhaps rage, in the core of my sadness. I was angry that Erik had been so careless in his driving that he killed my beautiful son. I was angry that he never contacted us afterwards to express remorse or sorrow, and angry that, according to some reports I'd heard, he was continuing to be what I termed a "dead-ender"; someone without much going on in his life, few goals, and no passion to make a difference in the world or even in himself. I was angry that he stole my son's life, yet seemed not to be making the most of his own opportunity for a full life. I knew I needed to forgive him and pray for his future.

I was also angry with myself and felt a sense of shame and guilt. The week before Willie's death, I had been visiting schools in Vermont with my daughter and although I could have made it work, I decided not to spend the extra time and money to combine this trip with a trip to Maine to visit my sons at the ski training facility. This was one of my very few regrets with regard to Willie's life and death, and it haunted me a little bit. I knew I needed to forgive myself.

I was also haunted by a feeling that I had failed in my responsibility to God. I knew that one of the reasons for my being sent back to earth after my boating accident was to help support my family and, more specifically, help my husband deal with the death of our son. I was also meant to help them discover their relationship with God. I had tried my best, but in February 2010, I didn't think any of them were closer to God and Bill was still filled with a pervasive sense of despair. I felt empty and defeated. I was incapable of helping him, my kids, or myself.

As I listened to Father Ubald speak, I contemplated his loving and joyful manner. It then suddenly occurred to me that my sense of failure was self-inflicted and egocentric. I had stopped looking to God for help, believing that I was expected to do it all on my own. Believing that I **could** do it all on my own. In the process, I had let doubts, fear, and guilt silently creep in and take over my thoughts. I was still in the valley of the shadow of death and the door of my heart was propped wide open. Right then and there, I asked God for help and immediately felt forgiven and free, knowing that God was in control. I prayed for guidance, requesting that God would help our family move forward in the process of grieving, and prayed that Bill would begin to see a glimmer of hope for the future. Once again, I would say that God answered my prayers, though definitely not in the way I had imagined.

In our conversation on loss and forgiveness, Father Ubald identified Bill's sense of despair and, I think, my sense of failure. He noted that while sadness reflects love, despair reflects the destruction of the soul that often accompanies grief. He then got up from the table, filled a bowl with water, blessed the water, and proceeded to move throughout our home sprinkling this holy water on everything he saw . . . actually, **pouring handfuls of water** would be a more accurate description. He spread holy water in every area of every room, in every closet, and on every object and every surface . . . on everything everywhere. As he did so, he commanded that the evil of despair leave our home and leave our family.

I have never been a Catholic, so I am not sure what to think about holy water, but I do know one thing: Our lives changed after Father Ubald's visit. We still felt the sadness of loss, but the sense of fear and despair that had been slowly destroying our lives departed that evening.

Is it just "coincidental" that I broke my ankle at the time Father Ubald was visiting, or that I was too ill to speak with him in the hospital, thereby providing the opportunity for Father Ubald to bring healing to me, to Bill, and to our family? Perhaps it is, but I think it is more likely another example of God's perfectly and choreographed sequence of events.

CHAPTER 33

LOGICAL CONCLUSIONS

**"And now these three remain:
Faith, Hope, and Love.
But the greatest of these is Love."**

—1 Corinthians 13 (NIV)

༄

As I consider the story of my life, I recognize that each of my experiences has prepared me for the next one. There is a divine sequence and order to my life, and this sequence prepared me for my greatest challenge to date: the death of my son. Since his death, I continue to cling to my daily creed (the one taped to the fridge), because it reflects the convictions and logical conclusions I already know to be true based on my past experiences.

4. **I believe God's promises are true:** God promises not to leave us nor forsake us. God promises to open the door when we

knock, and to always welcome us back into
his love, no matter how far we have strayed.
In my life, He fulfilled these promises when
he brought George into my life, when He
was with me in the tumbling car, when He
showed me and my scuba instructor the way
out of the Florida cave, and when I drowned
on a South American river. He loved me even
when I was an angry adolescent and when I
let Him slip into the background of my life.
I could be confident that God had a plan for
Willie and for us.

5. **I believe heaven is real:** My patient Jennifer
saw the angels. My patient who died after
spinal surgery saw angels and described both
the angels and heaven to his wife. I experienced heaven first-hand after my kayaking
accident. The heaven I witnessed was so pure,
love-filled, and magnificent that I did not
want to return to earth. When my life still
hung in the balance, I was also reassured that
my husband and children would be "okay,"
even if I died. I have no doubt that Willie
was hesitant to leave his family behind and
sorry for what we would bear, but I also have
no doubt that he was similarly reassured before jubilantly returning to God.

6. **I believe nothing can separate me from
God's love:** God's love was present with me

when I was spinning out of control, when the truck was stuck in the mud in the middle of the Mexican mountains, as well as during the various times when I was anxious about my personal life or work situations. He held me and loved me when I was pinned in a waterfall and dying. He kept me from feeling pain or worry. The experience of His presence, love, and compassion reassures me that Willie suffered no pain at the end of his life. His spirit probably left his body long before it was broken, and I feel confident that he was greeted by a host of overjoyed and excited witnesses.

7. **I believe God has work for me to do:** While in the hospital after my boating accident, the angels talked about the work we all do on earth, and they discussed some specifics about the work I still needed to do. Clearly, Willie completed his job on earth. He lived passionately, he loved deeply, he achieved success, and he inspired others to become better people. He accomplished a great deal in his nineteen years and made this world a better place for all. He got the job done.

8. **I believe God will see me through and carry me when I cannot walk:** There are many cycles in a person's life, and everyone

experiences hurt, worry, disappointment, grief, and other difficulties. It has been said that one cannot truly appreciate joy without also experiencing sorrow. I had survived many sorrows before Willie's death, some minor and some major. God was with me for each one, carrying me forward until I was able to walk on my own and nurture the very small seed of hope for the future that He buries within each of us. This history allows me the certainly of knowing that no matter how devastated and doubtful of the future I may feel, God will always be there to walk with me and carry me into a joyful future. Each event, whether joyous or sorrowful, has given me greater awareness of God's role in my life and has led me to a deeper faith in God's unfailing love.

I still don't know what the future holds for me. I do not doubt God's promises and I am grateful for the privilege of having had Willie in our lives. He was a great teacher and role model, a great son and friend. Willie believed that change begins with the individual, and passionately embraced Mahatma Gandhi's idea: "We must be the change we wish to see in the world." In Willie's seemingly accelerated life on earth, he accomplished a great deal and inspired others to do the same. He showed others a better way of living.

He was certainly the change he wished to see in the world.

He knew who he was and what he stood for. He reached for his dreams. He was kind and always thought about others before himself. He expected each of us to look in the mirror every evening and ask what **we**, not someone else, have done **today** to help someone else or to make this world a better place for all.

I do not believe that a loss of the magnitude I've experienced in losing Willie is something a person "gets beyond," "works through," or any of those other well-meaning, but impossible-to-achieve platitudes. Grieving a loss is a matter of learning to incorporate the pain into a new life and a new reality. As Martha Hickman wrote in her book **Healing after Loss** (HarperCollins, 2009), "There is no way out, only forward."

Many have said that my experience is remarkable. Perhaps it is. What I find more remarkable, however, is how readily many people in our society believe outlandish and unsubstantiated urban myths and conspiracies (Pop Rocks and Coke, JKF assassination, AIDS is man-made, etc.), yet disregard thousands of personal and consistent testimonies of miracles and near-death experiences from people throughout all cultures and religions.

I have spent more than ten years reflecting on my experiences and wondering what I am meant to do with them. In this process, I have continued to be what I have always been: a wife and mother, a spine surgeon, a scientist, a realist, and a cynic, yet I am profoundly changed. I know that above all else, I am a child of God. I know that God loves and values each person on earth. I know that we are each only small threads in God's glorious tapestry, but I also know that our choices and our actions are important and really do make a difference.

This knowledge has changed the way I interact with my medical patients. I recognize how significantly a patient's emotional and spiritual health impacts their recovery and I am able to use my own experiences to give them hope, even in the midst of substantial disability or injury. I often pray for my patients and, occasionally, with them. I now see my professional role as more of a "healer" rather than of someone who just "fixes" their mechanical problem.

I do not know why God chose to intervene in my life. I have led a very ordinary life. I was raised with religion but never truly claimed God's promises for myself until I was in high school. I spent little time thinking about my spiritual life when I was an undergraduate student, even though I believe God intervened in my life when I was scuba diving in the Florida Springs. I could say the same for my time in medical school and residency. Like many people, I was consumed by the details and obligations of daily life and by the familiar challenge of balancing the needs of work, marriage, and children. Despite being personally touched by God's presence in my life, my spirituality did not begin to blossom until I thought about what I wanted for my children.

Since I feel quite ordinary in so many ways, I continue to ask the ordinary question, "Why me?" Why did God choose to give me these extraordinary experiences instead of showing Himself to my cousin who died in the talons of drug addiction or to any of the millions of other believers on earth who have cried out for His help? I am analytical, scientific, and skeptical by nature and by training. I'm not sure I would believe all the events of my life's story to be true if I had not personally lived each day of them. How can all that I have described happen in one person's life, and why is it so to stop doubting and just believe?

I do not know all of the answers to these questions, but I do know that millions of people are in dire need of knowing God, receiving His love, experiencing His presence, and accepting the truth of His promises.

People ask why so many miracles occurred in ancient days but not in our present time. I contend that there are just as many miracles occurring today, in the lives of ordinary people. But I also assert that most of us don't look for miracles, don't recognize them for what they really are, and don't really believe them to be of divine origin even if their miraculous nature is noticed.

My life's experiences would argue against the concepts of coincidence and luck. It would support the belief that there is only the guiding presence and plan of God, who uses His assortment of angels and messengers to lead us and communicate with us.

King Solomon wrote in Ecclesiastes that "people cannot see the whole scope of God's work from beginning to end" and I would heartily agree. We live our lives in forward motion, but only understand them when looking backward. I therefore challenge you to keep a six- to twelve-month journal of coincidence. In that journal, write down the details of every "coincidence" you experience. In one column, write the details of each major event in your life . . . What are/were the circumstances surrounding your acceptance into college, meeting your significant other, finding your job, choosing where you live, and so on. Note every time the arrangements easily fall into place. Similarly, every time you struggle with a situation write down the eventual outcome. Write down the "bad" things that happen to you or others and, in an adjacent column, list what happens as a direct or indirect result of these bad things. I believe that when you look back through your journal at the end of your exercise, you will clearly see how many of people, events, decisions, and outcomes are interconnected. I think you will see a pattern of linkage that cannot be attributed to statistical chance. You will see evidence of God's work in your life, giving assurance that God has a plan for your life. You will begin to recognize coincidental events for the miracles they really are, and you will know that God is with you even in times of sorrow, loneliness, or other misfortune. To paraphrase what Chad Long once said: "Let's not let life muddle what happens. We are all part of a miracle."

It is written in **Hebrews 11:1, (NIV)**: "Faith is being sure of what we hoped for and certain of what we do not see." Martin Luther King, Jr., translated this into the world of action when he stated: **"Faith is taking the first step even when you don't see the whole staircase."**

It is this faith that sets us free. It allows us to fully embrace life, dissolves fear, and replaces worry with hope. Faith allows us to confidently walk with God into a future filled with joy; one that can become an extraordinary and amazing adventure.

God created us, knows us, loves us, and guides us. With love and grace, He commands us to:

- Rejoice in this knowledge always.

- Live a life of prayer, giving glory to God and continually listening for His guidance.

- Live a life of gratitude, giving thanks in all circumstances.

GIVING BACK

**"You can give without loving,
but you cannot love without giving."**

—Amy Carmichael

A portion of the proceeds from the sale of this book will be given to charitable organizations that strive to:

- Share God's grace and love in our country and the world.

- Encourage individuals to make each day and each choice matter, and to work to make the world a better place for all.

- Promote responsible stewardship of the world that has been given to us.

- Help bring people into a loving relationship with God.

For further information, please visit:

www.DrMaryNeal.com

On this website, you will find information about the specific non-profit organizations to which donations are made. You will also find a means by which you can suggest other non-profit organizations that should be considered.

Q&A WITH DR. NEAL

❧

Since the publication of my book, I have answered many questions about the details of my experiences. Some of the most frequently asked questions are addressed below.

Where is Jesus in this story?

I believe Jesus was holding me, comforting me, and reassuring me when I was drowning. I also believe that it was with Jesus I was conversing when sitting in the beautiful field during my out-of-body experiences. I did not clearly state this when I wrote the first edition of my book because I still felt uncomfortable with this claim. I am an ordinary person, and it seemed so presumptuous and arrogant to think that Jesus would take the time to be with me.

Do you belong to a church?

I regularly attend church services and have served on the board of elders, but I believe that loving the Lord your God with all your heart, soul, and strength is of the greatest importance. I live in a beautiful and mountainous area and many people claim the mountains as their church and believe they can worship God there instead of within a building. That can certainly be true but the question, as is often posed by my pastor, is not can a person worship God while in the mountains, but will that person worship God while in the mountains? Regardless of the harm that some individuals have done in the name of God or while hiding behind the doors of the church, I believe the institution is greater than the individuals within it. Churches provide a place of gathering for people who share common beliefs, support and encouragement for each other in faith, a place to find insight into and teaching about God's Word, and they provide a time and place where people can leave the world behind and focus only on their spiritual relationship with God. Just as God can meet us wherever we are, the variety of denominations allows for accommodation of people in all stages of spiritual growth.

Are you just doing this for the money?

I, too, am skeptical of the motivation of many people, but God has given me these experiences for a purpose, and I am trying to be obedient to what He has asked of me. Proceeds from the sale of this book help support several non-profit organizations (the current list of charities supported can be found on the "Giving Back" page of my website).

Why did it take so long to write your book?

I believe that the fact that I really, really did not want to return to earth is an important part of my story. At the time of my kayaking accident, my four children were quite young, and other than telling my close friends and church about it, I didn't speak much about my experiences because I never wanted my children to think that they weren't enough of a reason for me to come back. I was a surgeon, wife, and mother of four, which did not allow much time for writing, and, frankly, I didn't want to do it. I was not a writer and was a very private person. Ultimately, God's timing is always perfect; I finished writing the first complete draft hours before my son's death.

Why should I believe you? Aren't you just trying to convince people of your way of believing?

The job I was given was to share my experiences as accurately and precisely as I can. This is all I am trying to do.

What did the people look like who were with you in heaven?

The people/beings were brilliant. They had physical form but seemed to be wearing flowing robes such that I did not see distinct arms or legs. I did see their heads, but their brilliance seemed to blur the edges such that their features were indistinct. They seemed neither young nor old—just timeless. When I had my out-of-body experiences while in intensive care, I saw children playing at the far end of the field in which I was sitting.

What did Jesus look like?

I believe Jesus was holding me when I was still underwater. At that point I heard Him speaking to me but did not see Him. I believe it was Jesus with whom I was conversing in the sun-kissed field during my later out-of-body experiences. He was sitting on a rock while I was sitting on the ground and, like the people who led me down the path to heaven, He was wearing some sort of flowing robe and exploded with beauty and brilliance. His hair was long. His features were indistinct. I don't know how to describe this but my greatest impression of His appearance was that of love (yes, I realize we don't typically "see" love, but as I said, I don't know how to describe this phenomenon of "seeing" something we would normally "feel"). He conveyed the impression of complete love, compassion, kindness, and infinite patience.

Did you see pets?

I did not see animals, but I experienced only a couple of places and have no idea about the things and places I did not experience.

What were your injuries, and why didn't you arrange for a medical evacuation?

I am surprised that readers have wanted to know the details of my injuries, but here they are: In one leg, I suffered a tibial plateau fracture, a meniscal tear, and tears of the posterior cruciate ligament, the posterior capsule, and the collateral ligaments of my knee. In the other leg, I suffered a proximal tibia and fibula fracture, and tears of the posterior capsule and collateral ligaments, and a stretch of the posterior cruciate ligament. Basically, my knees bent entirely backward upon themselves in order for my body to exit the kayak. By the time I arrived in the emergency room, I also had developed pneumonia and severe respiratory distress syndrome (basically a shock reaction of the lungs to trauma), which is a condition that dramatically decreases the ability of the lungs to transfer oxygen to the bloodstream. Supplemental oxygen and supportive care are important, but other than allowing time for the lungs to heal, there is no particularly effective treatment for this condition, and it often leads to death. I initially had oxygen saturation levels in the 40s (normal levels should be 80–100), increasing to the 60s with supplemental oxygen. Generally, these levels are not sustainable without expecting severe organ damage. I developed deep venous thrombosis in my legs, which required anticoagulation, and I underwent multiple surgeries and extensive rehabilitation. I did not suffer brain injury, and eventually my legs healed as well as could be expected; I certainly live with the long-term consequences of my physical injuries, but I have been able to return to many physical recreational activities.

We should have called for a medical evacuation. Although it turned out "okay" for me, it was foolish and ill conceived, and not something I would ever recommend. I had decided to fly home to be with my children, and I rationalized that because I was a doctor, my legs had been splinted, and I would be traveling with another physician (my husband), all would be fine. However, I was certainly in a state of shock and felt little connection to the cares of this world; my husband was in a state of shock too. Someone could have told us we were not thinking clearly, but we were the only physicians, and I think everyone deferred to our judgment (or lack thereof). Frankly, I am embarrassed by this part of my story.

What was your faith like before your kayaking accident, and how did your spiritual life change afterward?

Before my near-death experience, I was a Christian and believed that the Bible was the absolute and historically accurate Word of God. I was not, however, what anyone would call deeply spiritual or deeply religious and had no preconceived notions about life after death. My experience changed me profoundly in both spiritual and religious ways. I now know the promises of God to be true, that there is a life after death, and our spiritual life is eternal. While recognizing the limitations of organized religion, I fully participate in and support it.

How has your understanding of God changed?

The absolute knowledge that God is real, that He has a plan for each of us, and that there really is life after death changes the way I experience each day. I do not fear death, and that also changes the way I experience the death of others, even my own son. I know that every day really does matter and that I need to be about God's business every day. I also know that God loves all people deeply and unconditionally . . . even those people whom I may not like or agree with. It motivates me to try to see the beauty in them that God sees.

How can these experiences be applied to others or used to face challenges?

I have given many details of my life not so that anyone should try to replicate them, but to show others that if you can transform your faith into trust, you can face any challenge with a grateful and joyful heart. What I mean is this: a small child has hope—hope that God will do what He says He will do. When we hear about and see God working in the lives of others, that hope transforms into a faith that God will really do what He says He will do. Not everyone has a profound spiritual experience such as a near-death experience, but taking the time to really look at the patterns of your everyday life and noting how events seem to unfold in a manner that is unlikely a result of chance allow any person of faith to begin to see God working in his own life. I think it is only when a person truly sees God working in his own life that this faith can be transformed into a complete trust that God's promises are true. Complete trust that God has a beautiful plan and that it is one with a hope and a future allows me, and each of us, to face challenges with confidence and courage, even when the plan and its beauty seem hidden.

ABOUT THE AUTHOR

᠎

**Mary C. Neal, MD,** is a board-certified orthopædic surgeon, former director of spine surgery at the University of Southern California, and a founding partner of Orthopædic Associates of Jackson Hole, Wyoming. She received her medical degree from the University of California at Los Angeles School of Medicine, where she also trained in general surgery before completing an orthopædic surgery residency at the University of Southern California. She went on to complete three fellowships in spinal surgery, trauma, and spine rehabilitation at highly-respected hospitals in Sweden, Switzerland, and California. Dr. Neal has published multiple articles and book chapters, and is a member of numerous medical professional associations in the United States.

Dr. Neal is committed to the causes of environmental stewardship, individual responsibility for making the world a better place, and increasing awareness of God's presence, love and grace. She has served as an elder in the Presbyterian Church of Jackson Hole, as a member of the board of directors for several non-profit organizations, and created the Willie Neal Environmental Awareness Fund (wnealenvirofund.org).

An avid sportswoman, Dr. Neal participates in recreational and competitive skiing, kayaking, bicycling, as do her husband, William C. Neal, MD, and their children. In 1999, while on vacation kayaking in the Los Ríos region of southern Chile, she became trapped inside a waterfall and drowned. Before being resuscitated, she had a remarkable, joyful experience of going to heaven and engaging in direct communication with angels. As an inspirational speaker, she lectures publicly about this transformational event and how it has impacted her life and her family, as well as the important lessons it holds about the meaning and purpose of our lives.